Praise for *Gather*

Healing ministry is an untapped reservoir of the church. The church must explore it in every possible way to represent the healing presence of Christ in our broken world.

Tilda Norberg gives creative voice to the church's calling to liturgically honor and appropriate God's gracious movement toward healing and wholeness, one person at a time. *Gathered Together* is a generous gift to the church from an exceptionally insightful, wise, and gifted pastor.

—JEREMIAH J. PARK
Resident Bishop, New York Area
The United Methodist Church

Pastors should feel at home with this book; laypersons should feel empowered by it. *Gathered Together* is a splendid contribution to the field of spiritual counseling.

—REV. JOHN J. KING, SJ
Retreat Minister, Mount Manresa Jesuit Retreat House
Staten Island, New York

Tilda Norberg agrees with the tenet of Gestalt theory that humans have an innate yearning to grow and heal. She adds her belief that Jesus wants us to attain both objectives.

In *Gathered Together* Norberg shows how symbols and keen intuition can facilitate the healing process. She calls on the power of simple Christian symbols and rites like Eucharist, baptism, anointing, laying on of hands, foot washing, and chanting. Importantly, she encourages "gathering together" supportive friends to join in prayer for the person in need. This book reports remarkable examples of healing and transformation as the result of such "personal liturgies."

—HUGUES J. P. RYSER, MD
Professor Emeritus, Boston University School of Medicine

Gathered Together is essential reading for anyone seeking to understand and practice healing ministry. Joining stories, psychological insight, theological reflection, and practices of healing prayer for individuals, *Gathered Together* provides individuals and healing teams with resources to promote the healing of persons in need. The book sets forth a step-by-step approach for creating liturgies for personal healing that can be readily adapted.

This book will enable churches to embody a truly holistic ministry of healing that embraces healing prayer for individual transformation as well as congregational worship. It will help healing teams understand the psychological dimensions of illness and the trauma of persons in pain. *Gathered Together* will awaken your congregation's experience of God's healing touch through individual as well as community prayer and ritual.

—BRUCE G. EPPERLY
Professor of Practical Theology, Lancaster Theological Seminary
Author of *God's Touch: Faith, Wholeness, and the Healing Miracles of Jesus*
and *Healing Worship: Purpose and Practice*

Tilda Norberg documents story after story of personal liturgy experiences in which the Holy Spirit breaks forth in powerful, awe-inspiring ways. *Gathered Together* is a ministry resource that invites pastors, prayer teams, and laity into the artfully organic and grace-filled process of creating personal liturgies that bless, transform, and heal.

—THE REVEREND ANNE M. CORMIER, MDIV, MSW, LSW
Gestalt Pastoral Care Minister

I find *Gathered Together* a great asset in the work I do in churches and in retreat centers. Rather than providing an off-the-rack healing prayer that may not exactly fit the person/situation, this book provides the components to construct, shape, and create a tailor-made healing liturgy specific to the needs presented by the person/situation I am working with at the time.

—SISTER ANNA TANTSITS, IHM
Retreat team, Franciscan Ministry of the Word at Bethany Ministries
Former Associate Director for Adult Faith Formation & Evangelization
for the Diocese of Albany

Gathered Together

Creating Personal Liturgies
for Healing and Transformation

Tilda Norberg

UPPER
ROOM BOOKS®
NASHVILLE

GATHERED TOGETHER
Creating Personal Liturgies for Healing and Transformation
© Copyright 2007 by Tilda Norberg
All rights reserved.

Cover design: Left Coast Design, Portland, Oregon
Cover image: Fancy Photography collection, Veer.com
Interior design: Nancy Terzian / NTer Design, Nashville, TN
Author photo: Thomas Duncan Photography
First printing: 2007

Library of Congress Cataloging-in-Publication
Norberg, Tilda.
Gathered together : creating personal liturgies for healing and transformation / Tilda Norberg.
    p. cm.
Includes bibliographical references.
ISBN 978-0-8358-9916-1
1. Liturgies. 2. Spiritual healing. I. Title.
BV178.N67 2007
265'.9—dc22
                              2007000450
Printed in the United States of America

For Silas Gray Norberg Bodah, already a lover of books.

Thanks again to Noah, Shana, Dan, and, of course, George.
I cherish each of you.

I am always grateful for the encouragement and support of the
members of Gestalt Pastoral Care Ecumenical Associates,
excellent women all: Anne Cormier, Wanda Craner,
Rhoda Glick, and Sara Goold.

And to those people who allowed their stories to be told,
special thanks for your faith and generosity.

Contents

Introduction   9

Chapter 1   Liturgies: Vehicles of Healing   17
Chapter 2   What Are Personal Healing Liturgies?   33
Chapter 3   Opportunities for Personal Healing Liturgies   43
Chapter 4   Getting Ready to Lead a Personal Healing Liturgy   61
Chapter 5   Leading a Personal Healing Liturgy   77

Stories of Personal Healing Liturgies   93

   Liturgies of Celebration   95
        Finding Roots   95
        Recovery from Cancer   98

   Rites of Passage   101
        Jessica's Vows   101
        Becoming a Man   103
        A Service of Endings and Beginnings   109

   Liturgies of Vocational Blessing   114
        A Ministry of Car Repair   114
        The Dedication of a Musical Career   115

Liturgies of Commissioning   117
   First Steps toward a New Project   117
   Becoming a Mennonite Wild Woman   121

Liturgies of Declaration   125
   Good Enough!   125
   Undoing Old Vows and Making New Ones   129
   Claiming Motherhood   131

Liturgies of Surrender   134
   Giving Up Family Shame and Sorrow   134
   Giving Up False Hope   136

Liturgies of Grieving   139
   A Funeral, One Year Later   139
   Creating a Memorial Shrine   140

Liturgies in Desolation   146
   Losing a Job, Gaining Hope   146
   Creating a Garden of Hope   147

Liturgies of Healing from Sexual Abuse   151
   Telling a Secret   151
   Pablo's Confession   154
   Tough Love   156
   Eileen's Cleansing   162
   Eileen's Celebration: Making Vows
     and Taking a New Name   168

Appendix: Naming Lies, Speaking the Truth   177
Notes   181
Bibliography and Resources   185
About the Author   187
About Gestalt Pastoral Care   190

Introduction

Liturgical creativity is blooming these days. Many churches are familiar with worship that incorporates dance, drama, video, computer-generated graphics, carefully written prayers replete with current concerns and vocabulary, specially written hymns, or artistically riveting settings for worship. Healing services targeting particular groups, such as the newly divorced, survivors of sexual abuse, or adoptive parents, or services focused around burning issues of justice and peace are often an important feature of these new liturgies.

Gathered Together both draws from the current liturgical renewal and branches off from it. This book focuses on the largely untapped resources of the church to create corporate liturgies of healing or celebration *for the benefit of just one person at a time*. Personalized healing liturgies serve as a bridge between pastoral care and the worship traditions of the church, and incorporate material from both Christian liturgical traditions and scripture, as well as one person's particular need for healing or growth.

Individualized liturgies recognize the deep involvement of countless church members in methods of personal growth outside the church. These persons attend 12-step groups or engage in personal journaling, artistic endeavors, or peer sharing. They read self-help books. They pursue alternative and holistic methods of healing for medical conditions. Some participate in private or group psychotherapy. Many church members could affirm that these individuals are working to grow, and that they are changing for the better. Even so, for committed Christians these good door-opening methods may feel oddly incomplete, for spiritual matters are often overtly ignored. In the secular context of many growth groups (excluding 12-step programs), any discussion of spirituality, especially Christian spirituality, is considered bad form or simply irrelevant.

Unfortunately, this particularly holds true for most forms of psychotherapy. Many people whose stories are told in this book have been helped greatly by psychotherapy. There they discovered their courage, their resilience, their very selves. Some would even say that psychotherapy saved their lives. However, only a few have experienced a therapist who can and will respond in depth to their Christian faith. For most, a great divide existed between spirit and emotion that both therapist and client knew they were not to breach.

Personal liturgies of healing are a unique contribution to an individual growth process that pastors and other ministering persons are best equipped to make.

Individualized healing liturgies are not psychotherapy but a wonderful *adjunct* to an inner journey that may include therapy. Personal liturgies can bring closure to a process of secular psychotherapy or another growth modality, and occasionally even provide the missing element when a growth process stagnates. Sometimes growth stops precisely because a spiritual issue has not been addressed!

Personal liturgies of healing are a unique contribution to an individual growth process that pastors and other ministering persons are best equipped to make. After all, clergy are professionals specifically trained to create and lead liturgies, and nonordained ministers of healing likely have long experience with them as well. Creating liturgies is part of the church's special expertise. Further, Christians have an exceedingly rich tradition from which to draw, and pastors are the ones most likely to know about the many liturgies of the church through two thousand years of history. The prayers, the ancient and new practices, the many styles of worship are ours to claim and to set in new contexts.[1]

Thus, planning and leading these small, individualized liturgies is a way pastors and other ministering people can bring a vital component to the growth of parishioners. Individualized liturgies are a wonderful way to support both those just beginning a conscious growth process, as well as those who are emotionally and spiritually mature. I believe that individualized liturgies offer an exciting, effective, even necessary, contribution to personal growth—a natural addition to various healing ministries.

Because individualized liturgies draw heavily on the rich networks of friends, family members, prayer partners, and informal mentors found in most churches, they challenge members of existing support systems to minister personally and genuinely to one another. These liturgies model a vital way of *being church*, which could be described as midwifing one another's personal growth journey. As these liturgies take hold in a congregation, the pastor may find that she or he no longer does all the pastoral care. Laypeople are brought in quite naturally as they participate both informally and liturgically in one another's healing. Because these groups are fluid, configuring and disbanding in response to the needs of the moment, and because they become "church" for the recipient of the liturgy, I call them *ad hoc churches* or *ad hoc congregations.*

With wise and sensitive pastoral preparation, creative and effective liturgies can be planned around almost any life transition, growth milestone, or need for healing. Personal liturgies can gather an individual's growth experiences and recognize that the Holy One was indeed at work. They can help articulate the personally discovered meaning of suffering and become an arena for deeper engagement and commitment in a spiritual journey. They can proclaim in a meaningful way for the individual that "the light shines in the darkness, and the darkness did not overcome it" (John 1:5). Despite physical and emotional abuse that sent a message of shame and worthlessness, personal liturgies can powerfully affirm or even help construct a new, healthier self-identity. In the face of previous selfish and destructive lifestyles, a personal liturgy can proclaim forgiveness and invitation to joy in a way the recipient might be able to take in.

- Imagine a liturgy in which a prodigal son or daughter, tired of carrying around guilt, confesses sin one more time, then drops a heavy object on the floor to symbolize dropping the burden of guilt. Afterward a few good friends dress the prodigal in a "celebration outfit," which he or she wears for Eucharist and the subsequent party.

- Imagine a liturgical celebration attended by family members and a few friends to mark one person's long and hard-won sobriety.

- Imagine a special prayer service for a not-so-very-young woman who, after careful discernment, feels called to pursue a college degree in a new field.

- Imagine a group of church folk gathered for a special healing service for someone newly diagnosed with cancer.

- Imagine the power of a healing liturgy for a man who has discovered the time has come to give up some dysfunctional ways of being a father.

- Imagine what it might mean to an older person retiring from a long career, or someone transferring to another part of the country, or someone starting a much more responsible job, to recognize and even commission these big transitions liturgically.

Ministers may protest that their church members wouldn't make themselves that vulnerable; they wouldn't want that much attention. They would be ashamed to let even close friends and family know of their inner struggles. They might even be embarrassed to attend such a service of a friend.

True, personal liturgies aren't for everyone, and they don't have to be. But from more than thirty years of private practice and of leading workshops in which personal liturgies were either featured or a component of the retreat, I believe that in most churches there are at least a few who already hunger for such a ministry. These individuals may not know to ask, but when a personal liturgy is proposed to them, the answer is usually an enthusiastic "Yes!" It is as if they had been waiting for a way to share even more deeply with close friends, and to integrate their inner growth with their faith journey.

Those invited to attend a personal healing service often are excited by the event and feel moved to request a liturgy of their own. Thus, a ministry of personal liturgies might grow slowly and quietly among those who are ready. Pastors who have adopted such a ministry find that personally tailored services are a good way to ignite hunger for spiritual growth in those who already feel such stirrings.

Actually, personal liturgies are not such a new idea. For centuries the church has engaged in corporate liturgies that focus on one or two persons at a time.

Actually, personal liturgies are not such a new idea. For centuries the church has engaged in corporate liturgies that focus on one or two persons at a time. Good examples are church weddings or baptisms that, while rooted in Christian tradition, are usually explicitly personalized as well. These liturgies name names, sometimes tell stories, and require careful preparation of the persons who are the focus. They can become life-changing highlights of a person's journey that are remembered in great detail by the recipient. Many couples recall their wedding vows when their marriages need help, and sometimes years later the wedding liturgy plays an important role in healing and renewal. Similarly, at special times, the church reminds members to "remember your baptism and be thankful."

I propose that the church simply widen the scope of personal liturgies to include other transitions, milestones, mistakes, vows, and needs for healing, surrender, or celebration. Rather than radically departing from tradition, personal liturgies claim even more deeply the familiar traditions of the church: Eucharist, baptismal renewal, and anointing; along with some practices not so familiar to Protestants, such as liturgical bowing, making the sign of the cross, and foot washing. I further suggest that personal liturgies be created using not only the liturgical resources of the church, but also incorporating the person's life history, worship and devotional style, perceptual preference, language patterns, and personal symbols and meanings. Additionally, I propose that we look outside church buildings for natural and personally meaningful worship settings. Finally, I suggest that we expand our ideas about what activities might occasionally be part of a liturgy—to include such physical actions as embracing or surrendering a symbolic object.

By now you may be thinking that personal liturgies are too time-consuming and complicated to consider with your already too-full agenda. You may worry that planning a well-personalized service will surely eat up a tremendous amount of time. Sometimes that is true. When the service incorporates unusual settings or complicated physical actions (such as hiking up a mountain), two or more hours can go into planning, in addition to leading the service itself. Even so, considering the profound healing that can occur both in the recipient and the other participants, I believe the time is well spent.

Keep in mind, though, that many personal services are simple and brief liturgical actions that can be conceived and carried out almost as quickly and naturally as opening a meeting with prayer. These practically spontaneous actions can easily occur in the context of church groups already meeting regularly. Liturgies that need a bit more time can be planned and carried out on a church retreat or a reflection day, or in a study group, prayer group, or healing team training event.

Creating brief liturgical actions requires the minister to cultivate a mind-set that watches for moments to emphasize or reframe with responsive liturgical actions. For example, in an administrative church meeting you might do any of the following:

- Invite the committee to touch a certain pew and pray for one who usually sits there.

- Light a candle at the beginning of a church meeting for someone in special need, pausing during the meeting to pray briefly for that person several times.

- Pass around the college or job application of one member. As each person holds the papers, he or she prays for the applicant.

- Pass around a picture or a small possession of someone in special need, formally making a commitment to pray for that person in the coming week.

- Practice laying on of hands as the need arises.

- Anoint someone facing surgery.

- Lift a symbolic object as a sign that the group will lift someone's particular concern in prayer.

- Ring the church bell to celebrate a job well done by a member of the committee.

- Give a grieving person a flowering plant while saying such liturgical words as: "We offer you this plant in the name of Christ as a sign of our caring and of God's love for you. We believe that God is especially present with you now. Let the flowers be an icon of hope for you. And please remember that we are here if you need us."

As you gain more experience with personal liturgies, you may find that you learn to think a bit outside the liturgical box. You will begin to have a feel for quickly evaluating pastoral situations and coming up with creative liturgical ideas that can be immediately carried out to encourage church folk to cooperate with grace.

Many of the liturgies in this book occurred on Opening to Grace healing prayer retreats, a regular venue for my ministry of Gestalt Pastoral Care.[2] I occasionally propose a personal liturgy in response to someone's need. If the potential recipient agrees, the planning is completed, usually in a few minutes, by the whole group of six to eight persons. Then the ad hoc church prays the liturgy, which may be altered a bit as the assembled groups pay attention to the recipient's inner process. I have helped plan and lead individual liturgies of healing and brief liturgical actions for many years, and I still find it remarkable that the same healing grace mediated through prayer and laying on of hands also seems to be evident here as well. Simply put, the healing Christ often works through these small, sometimes even clumsy, liturgical actions.

The personal examples described in this book spring from several sources. Most are accounts of actual events and are told just as they occurred, although names and some identifying details have been changed. In certain instances I have written composite stories, weaving together components from the experiences of several different individuals. I created a few stories to illustrate what might be possible when working with personal liturgies.

Although I describe many personal liturgies in this book, you will not find complete orders of worship to use as they appear. Instead I encourage you to listen carefully to those who need healing—and then get creative. Plan each liturgy with a specific person in mind. The following chapters offer many examples of personal liturgies and suggest how to put together a personal liturgy for a specific need.

Chapter 1

Liturgies: Vehicles of Healing

My eyes were opened to the healing power of liturgy years ago when I was a part-time chaplain at South Beach Psychiatric Center, a large state hospital on Staten Island. I especially liked leading worship at the hospital, except for one big problem. Patients freely and frequently interrupted, sometimes even derailing beyond rescue the flow of my carefully planned services.

I knew that the disruptions sprang from the profound suffering of mental illness, but I was perplexed about how to deal with them so that worship might be a meaningful experience. I tried hard to make the services relevant and engaging, but despite my best efforts, nothing I did seemed to work, and the services remained chaotic. The turning point came after the following dialogue took place during a service for patients:

> *Me:* The New Testament reading is from the Gospel of John.
> *Someone else:* My brother's name is John.
> *Another person:* I hate John!
> *A voice in the back:* I have to go to the john, right now!
> [Suddenly someone pounded a metal chair, making quite a racket, and the entire crowd shifted in their seats.]
> *Me:* Okay. Let's all try to be quiet now and listen to the Bible.

I had lost them again, and my response was, as usual, puny and inadequate. In desperation, the following week, I decided to try something that seemed daring and, some might say, pretty foolish. I remembered that the East Harlem Protestant Parish where I had worked during seminary held foot washings regularly, and everyone, from seminary professors to street people, loved them. Maybe a more interactive service might channel the many distractions.

Then again, foot washing might cause real bedlam. Many psychiatric patients react with fear or anger at being touched, and I would be the only staff person in the chapel. How would they respond to being touched in this very meaningful and tender way? And how would those consumed with self-hatred or grandiosity react to assuming the role of Jesus? Was I setting up a situation that might spark a group meltdown? Or would everyone just sit there in frozen unwillingness to participate? Or might foot washing be a way to reach these suffering people?

In the end it seemed worth a try. Without telling anyone what I was planning, I decided to make the already short service very brief, eliminating most of the liturgy I had been using. With an opening, a short introduction, and a simple closing, the service would mostly consist of an experience of foot washing. I would make clear that no one would be pressured to participate. Before the next service, I rounded up some hospital basins along with soap and towels and had the room set up for foot washing. With a knotted stomach, I waited for the patients.

From the beginning things were different. After several opening hymns and a prayer, I told—rather than read—the story of Jesus washing the feet of the disciples. Then I said:

"You're probably wondering why there are towels and wash basins right next to the altar. It's because today we're going to do something different. We're going to have the chance to imitate what Jesus did when he washed the feet of his friends. Don't worry; if you don't want to participate, you can just watch. It's okay, too, if you want to leave.

"Anyone who wants to try foot washing will be able to wash the feet of another person. You will also have the chance to allow your feet to be washed, just like the disciples. Remember that Jesus invited his friends to wash one another's feet, so it's all right to do this.

"If you do decide to let someone wash your feet, it might be a way of experiencing how very much God loves you. If you decide to wash someone else's feet, you might discover that God wants to love others through you. Or something else might happen that will help you feel better. If you want to try it, be as open as you can to what God might be doing to heal you."

When I finished, everyone was listening quite attentively. I had the distinct feeling that this was getting through, and to my utter surprise, everyone wanted to stay. They divided into pairs, took off their shoes, and began. I watched so I could be available to respond if need be.

The next few minutes were astonishing. From all around the chapel I heard little snuffles and sobs. Many were openly weeping, not with anguish or fear, but with soft, releasing tears, gentle tears of relief and perhaps even joy. Faces distorted with tension relaxed, and shoulders let go. Rare smiles appeared. Deep peace seemed to pervade all of us, and for at least fifteen minutes no one did or said anything out of line. The chapel was pregnant with hope and relief. God's presence was quite evident, and we knew it.

A prayer of thanksgiving, a hymn, and the benediction ended the service, but no one wanted to leave. They all lingered until I reluctantly shooed them out for their dinner. Going out the door, they still were chatting easily and animatedly, like any group of adult friends. I was amazed and awed. I saw that God had worked in us deeply through the vehicle of this unfamiliar but simple Christian liturgical practice, calling forth the sanity long hidden under debilitating mental illness.[1]

Did the healing last? Not really. The fog of mental illness closed in again for most of them. Some seemed a bit improved, at least to me. But I like to think that most had received a gift of hope, the memory of a time when the thick curtains of confusion opened and they could remember what normal felt like. Perhaps it gave some a new impetus to fight for health rather than slide into uneasy capitulation to their illness. For me, besides seeing plain evidence of God's power, I learned that there was health even in very sick people. I witnessed the power of liturgy to touch human hearts.

I further discovered that I had plenty of disconcerting questions about what happened that day. What should I learn from this remarkable event? Was it just dumb luck and serendipity that I hit on the idea of foot washing, or was it really God's direction? (In retrospect, it surely seems like the specific leading of the Holy Spirit!) If it was God, was the experience simply a gift of surprising grace given for that day? Could it have been the novelty itself that partially provided the spark, or was I simply more present than usual as I led the service? Could I somehow make room for this marvelous outpouring of healing love and human clarity again?

Pondering these questions led to subsequent explorations with foot washing and some of the other healing liturgies shared throughout this book. In contrast to the hospital foot-washing service, the liturgies presented here are not planned primarily with the needs of a group in mind. Instead, each was specially created to assist the growth journey of a certain individual at a particular time.

As a United Methodist clergyperson, I have been appointed to a holistic healing ministry I have named Gestalt Pastoral Care. Although I lead many retreats and various training events, for years most of my work has been with individuals. The nature of this work with one person at a time has provided both the structures and the spaciousness to explore the possibilities of individualized liturgies. It has become increasingly clear that services involving a few people, who focus on the specific needs of one person, are a way that God often chooses to heal. The same healing grace that is poured out with laying on of hands and prayer also becomes evident in liturgies grounded both in church tradition and a particular need in one person's life.

To explain how Gestalt Pastoral Care gravitated naturally to the use of individualized healing liturgies, I must tell you a bit about

Gestalt. Gestalt work focuses not on analysis but on increased awareness of *what is going on right now*. Seldom do we talk *about* anything for long; rather, the minister tries to suggest how whatever is at issue can be *experienced* in the here and now. One of the ways this is accomplished is with the use of *Gestalt experiments.*

In Gestalt work, the focus is not on analysis but on increasing awareness of what is going on right now.

For example, if someone is recalling a memory of his aunt when he was six years old, I might ask him if, for a few minutes, he would be willing to let himself be six again and invite his aunt to be present in his imagination. Is he willing to speak *to* her rather than talk *about* her? Or perhaps a person comes in feeling sad and weepy. I might ask her if she will allow herself the awareness of where in her body sadness and weepiness are located. Is she willing to let that part of her body speak some words? make a sound or motion?

Experiments invite a seeker to try out a particular behavior while staying as aware as possible. Whatever comes to awareness can easily lead to new discoveries and more experiments involving body, mind, social milieu, or spirit. I have long been convinced that God heals through such awareness and action.[2]

Since I work mostly with church folk, it seemed natural to begin suggesting experiments that incorporated prayer or liturgical elements. I found myself saying things like: "Would you be willing to invite Jesus here and tell him what you just discovered a minute ago? See how he responds, will you?" or: "How would you like to bring a few good friends next time and let them witness liturgically to your increasing clarity that it is impossible to change your mother? Maybe together we could instead commend her to God's care. And if you want, all of us could pray for you." People took to these small liturgies right away. Many reported that they were profoundly significant and powerful.

Over the years I concluded that the church, with its rich liturgical tradition and its clergy already trained to adapt or create new ways of worship, has a vital and largely unexplored treasure to bring to the healing ministry. Furthermore, I'm convinced that now is the time for this ministry to come forth.

Christian Healing: The New Ministry

In recent years the church has experienced a major shift in awareness. Forty years ago, only a few pastors in Catholic and mainstream Protestant churches had discovered that the healing ministry of Jesus still continues. Most had only an inkling of the new (and ancient) holistic outlook that is now seeping into our collective consciousness.

Now a new bonfire has been ignited, a bonfire that has swept into churches of varied denominations. Many congregations have instituted healing services or trained small groups to pray for healing when someone is sick. They are adopting a more holistic approach to healing, understanding that many factors of body, mind, and spirit intersect when someone feels rotten. Theologies of healing have become more nuanced, and healing ministries have become no less faithful but more careful. Gone are the days when the guilt-producing refrain "If only you have enough faith, God will heal you" was the simplistic gist of many sermons on healing. Retreats on healing ministry are of great interest and meet an expanding need. Good books on healing abound. Quite a few pastors routinely pray for healing during counseling or in times of crisis, and many carry anointing oil as they go about their work. Countless church folk can personally attest that God heals in response to prayer. Across the

Gone are the days when the guilt-producing refrain "If only you have enough faith, God will heal you" was the simplistic gist of many a sermon on healing.

church, experiences of healing have been powerful catalysts for deepening faith and commitment, and have equipped members to better engage in ministries of service. The healing ministry is here to stay.

Healing: A Lifelong, Holistic Process

Having been involved in healing ministry for many years, I have often seen firsthand the marvelous healing of God. Like many others, I have had to work my way to an understanding of Christian healing that seems consistent with scripture, psychology, medicine, and, most certainly, the experience of people who have prayed for healing.

I believe that it is *God's nature to heal,* that is, to continue creating us to be the unique persons God intends. When we are sick; when disaster strikes; when we are buffeted by betrayal, tragedy, abuse, or our own sin; when we are oppressed by distorted social systems, God's desire is to redeem, transform, and make new. We are saved, redeemed, and born again not just once but repeatedly throughout our lives as we are invited to grow in grace. This growth continues whether we are old or young, renegade or saintly, overtly suffering or feeling pretty well. We can trust that God is always inviting us to the next step in our growth and healing, even at death. At every stage, age, and circumstance in our lives, God nudges us to grow and change.

God's healing is not only *constant and lifelong* but also *holistic.* Remember, the healing miracles of Jesus were not just physical, although we tend to read the Gospel stories as if they were. Think about it: when Jesus touched people, they were transformed physically, emotionally, spiritually, cognitively, vocationally, and socially. They were set free for a new way of life that involved every level of their being. Often they were healed in surprising ways and sometimes not quite the way they had envisioned. Whether in biblical times or today, instant or rapid healing sets up the need for profound adjustments of every kind, making room for a host of new understandings, emotions, spiritual surrender, challenges, and obligations. Dramatic stories of sudden healing usually don't begin to tell the whole tale; the process that occurs before and after is often omitted in the telling.

Consider the story in Mark 2:1-12 and Luke 5:17-26 of the paralyzed man lowered through the roof by his nervy friends. This story shines with the holistic approach of Jesus. Jesus healed the man *spiritually* by forgiving his sins, and *physically* by curing his paralysis. Strongly implied is that the man was dramatically healed *emotionally* as well; he quickly somersaulted from hopelessness and despair to joyful awe. He must have been touched *cognitively*, as he listened to Jesus' dialogue with the critical scribes and heard a brand-new theology of God's love. He was challenged to adjust *socially*, going from helplessness to initiative, beginning with carrying his own bed home. Suddenly he was both gifted and burdened with new responsibilities: he had to earn a living, pull his weight in friendships, learn to do for himself. Perhaps he felt other reverberations as he realized that Jesus, the important rabbi, was willing to pay attention to his sorry self. It doesn't take much imagination to guess that his body, mind, emotions, spirit, and sociability were in an exciting and scary uproar as he took his first steps into a new way of life.[3]

The healing love of Christ continues to be holistic. Sometimes we pray to be healed in a certain way, and we discover that God seems to be working with a completely different area first. Why? Because we are created as whole beings. We moderns are rediscovering what the ancients knew well: when something is wrong, every part of us is affected. Whether we complain that we are physically sick, emotionally adrift, spiritually bereft, or socially oppressed, we respond with every part of ourselves: body, emotions, mind, spirit, and sociability. As we pray for continued healing, we may well be challenged to attend to each of these realms. My longtime experience in the healing ministry has taught me that human beings are wired for lifelong growth in which God shapes each person's healing individually and uniquely, weaving in and out of each part of our being.

Thus, healing is always a *process*. True, sometimes people pray for major healing and are instantly and dramatically healed, just as they were in New Testament times. I have witnessed such marvels on occasion, and it is wonderful indeed. However, most who are healed from serious illness experience a holistic process that is longer and more gradual.

A healing process is a moving, elating, wondrous, and sometimes an admittedly scary journey inviting us forward. Scary, because healing can take us into areas we may not wish to enter. When we long to be healed immediately of what pains us the most, we may be impatient or unwilling to attend to other areas. Say, for example, a woman finds out she has cancer. Naturally her prayers would focus around her desire to be healed physically. However, as she prays for physical healing, the way ahead might be through a veritable maze that zigzags into every aspect of her existence. Over time she might be led to

> give up an old grudge,
> offer forgiveness,
> confess a sin,
> cooperate with her doctor or find a new one,
> surrender an expectation of just how healing will occur,
> get involved with the poor,
> embrace a new self-identity,
> admit to an addiction,
> commit to increased rest and exercise,
> reframe an old memory,
> stop controlling her family,
> eat wisely, and
> continue to pray for physical healing.

In my experience, engaging with such a holistic process is frequently accompanied by physical improvement and sometimes complete physical healing. There are, however, many places to get stuck or detoured on such a journey. We can simply stop consenting to the grace that calls us forward. We can easily dig in our heels and stop our healing process, settling down where we have landed. We find ways to get comfortable with half measures. Then inertia sets in; fear takes over; social pressure multiplies; habits ossify; and pride obstructs progress. This can be true even if part of us still yearns for genuine transformation.

When we pray for healing, it seems that this easily blocked, complex inner process can get untangled and greatly speeded up. Awareness shifts and broadens; the steps become clearer; and we become more ready and able to welcome healing grace. This inner process, directed toward bringing us to "to maturity, to the measure of the full stature of Christ" (Eph. 4:13), is beautifully orchestrated by God, as we keep cooperating as best we can.

Naturally, we can't compel God to act on our timetable. Despite our earnest prayers and our best willingness to surrender to whatever healing God wants, it may seem that God has put the process on hold.

Naturally, we can't compel God to act on our timetable. Despite our earnest prayers and best willingness to surrender to whatever healing God wants, it may seem that God has put the process on hold. It may even seem that God has gone somewhere else. At this juncture it's important not to blame or beat ourselves up but to stay open as best we can. We can also ask ourselves if a small part of us just might stand in the way of our surrender.

Good pastoral care proves helpful at these "stuck" times, when people prayerfully ask how they might be stopping themselves. In this context, Christian liturgies that are planned specifically to target one person's need for healing can be powerful vehicles of grace. In fact, individualized liturgies can speak soul language in a way that is beyond words, beyond inner urgings, beyond rational explanations, beyond psychotherapy, even beyond the best pastoral care. Liturgies can touch us profoundly, especially those rooted in faith. Simply put, we are created as beings of ritual, and God chooses to work through rituals. Special liturgies of healing at appropriate times can help break up a logjam, solidify new resolves, celebrate and recognize gains, and support the process of growth.

Rituals: A Basic Human Impulse

Something in us hungers mightily to express itself in ritual, both religious and secular. In our own country, secular rituals are everywhere. The Girl Scouts have a prescribed ritual when a Brownie becomes a Girl Scout. The Fourth of July produces a spate of patriotic rituals. Schools, service clubs, professional associations, and self-help groups all engage in ritual. In New York City, where I live, we are especially aware of the way people from diverse ethnic traditions around the world preserve their cultural heritage through special rituals.

Ritual exists in every human culture, and it is part of what distinguishes humans from the rest of the animal kingdom. Although other animals engage in stylized, predictable ritualistic behavior in competition for food and sexual partners, only humans *create* rituals to express, for example, group identity and roles, community, passages to a new life stage, and, most importantly, religious meaning. Anthropologists tell us that creating rituals, especially religious rituals, is a basic mark of being human. Rituals are as natural to us as eating and sex. They are simply foundational.

For eons human beings have used the language of ritual to express the inexpressible, for in the end ordinary language by itself doesn't go far enough. We need art, music, poetry, dance, symbolic objects, physical actions, and pithy words formed into rituals and religious liturgies to represent our deepest longings and our relation to that which is infinitely larger than ourselves. Liturgies help us pay attention; they direct our awareness toward what is most true.

That liturgical actions are innate to humans was brought home to me one afternoon in an unlikely place: a huge IKEA furniture store in Elizabeth, New Jersey. The store was crowded; the aisles were full; babies were fussing in their strollers; shoppers were speaking, some quite loudly, in many languages. Distracted and in a hurry, I had dashed in to buy a set of sheets and get out of there.

Suddenly, above all the hubbub, a young child's voice emerged, saying, "Holy, holy, holy, Lord God of hosts, heaven and earth are full of your glory . . ." I spun around and saw a little boy, perhaps about seven, with a girl who I guessed to be no older than four, sitting together on a couch. The boy was smiling gently as he spoke slowly and reverently; the girl was listening intently and with shining eyes was gazing at the boy. The two of them, oblivious to the crowds of people streaming by, were wrapped in a protective cocoon of rapt attention and, yes, worship. No one else seemed to hear the children, nor did I see their parents nearby. I watched, fascinated, but they didn't notice me. The boy continued to recite the entire Communion liturgy as the tiny girl gave some of the liturgical responses. Together they shared pretend bread and wine.

I was slowed down, drawn in, and greatly moved. These kids were not really playing, nor were they showing off. I didn't doubt for one second that they were worshiping. Surely they didn't really understand what they were doing, but they were responding instinctively to the sacredness and power of the words and the presence of the Holy Spirit. Obviously they thought enough of the words they heard at worship services to memorize and repeat them. I was struck with the realization that these two children were doing what comes natural to all of us—responding to meaning that is beyond words—and they were doing it through the most treasured liturgy of the Christian church.

Rituals, no matter what the context, are usually communal; we need to share them with a group of people who use the same symbolic language. Sharing a liturgy among friends and family gives authority and substance to these profound longings. A wedding in which the couple makes vows in the presence of God, respected witnesses, and loved ones has much greater power and meaning than one night over dinner simply exchanging a promise to stick together.

Through liturgies and various secular rituals, we are ushered from one stage of life to another, from one identity to the next, and we recognize and celebrate these changes communally. In the Hispanic community, when a girl turns fifteen, she is given a *quinceaños* celebration, often in the church, to formally recognize her passage into womanhood. Usually the service begins with the girl dressed in childish shoes. My young friend Margarita Martínez wore bunny slippers at the start of her *quinceaños* day. Later she was solemnly presented with her first pair of high heels and a sophisticated woman's necklace. Margarita publicly thanked her parents for raising her, and vowed to dedicate her new adult life to God. Then came speeches from family and friends that challenged her to remain faithful to the promises she had just made, and welcomed her as a new adult. Before we went downstairs for a delicious Salvadoran meal, the gathered church promised to pray for her continued growth and maturity. This special celebration was a crucial milestone that Margarita will remember all her life.

Through ritual we learn to identify with a group and affirm who we are most deeply. Rituals can began to shape how we feel about ourselves. In Christian liturgies we receive again the message that

- as children of God, we are loved passionately;
- God wants to heal us in some way;
- we have somewhere to turn when life falls apart;
- we are never alone;
- God views even the humblest life as a gift to be cherished;
- God is in charge of the world;
- no matter how terrible our suffering, Christ can transform it; and
- God has given each of us something special to offer others.

If we could truly let all these truths sink into our souls, imagine how much of our pain would be eased and how free we would be to love more deeply! Liturgies, especially tailor-made ones, can provide an opening and a "language" for the gospel to take deeper root in us.

Liturgies can help provide a way for us to declare what we know to be the truth, even if the truth is at odds with how we feel. Liturgies can help us *separate* our faith from emotions—just because we feel at the moment that God is not there, this does not mean that we have lost our faith or that God has gone away. Liturgies can also help us *integrate* faith with emotions, because we learn that God is with us in our emotional reactions, no matter how unsavory they may be. Even when we have faith, for example, that God gives a new life after death, when a loved one dies, we are still flattened with grief and a devastating sense that the loved one is forever lost to us. We may be angry at God, unable to pray, and feel spiritually dead. A personalized funeral that remembers the life of our loved one and declares the promise of eternal life can be a great comfort. The liturgy takes us to a place that we cannot go by ourselves. The result can be a greatly deepened, grounded, and integrated faith that even in times of greatest despair, God is still with us.

Liturgies can help provide a way for us to declare what we know to be the truth, even if the truth is at odds with how we feel.

Obviously, not all rituals are positive ones. The human impulse to create rituals can be distorted to destroy rather than to build up, to ridicule rather than encourage, to exclude rather than embrace, or to glorify violence instead of tolerance. When fraternity and sorority rituals veer into extreme hazing, the result can be emotionally damaging and physically dangerous. Ku Klux Klan rituals that galvanize followers to commit hate crimes, and satanic rituals involving unimaginable cruelty are horrifying, convincing evidence that rituals are both powerful and subject to sin. The inherent power of ritual to shape consciousness and identity makes these practices particularly grotesque and dangerous. Life-sapping rituals can be so destructive that the very word *ritual* frightens some survivors. For this reason I have chosen to use the words *liturgy* and *service* to describe the Christian practices in this book.

Given that rituals are innate for human beings, and that they are important in establishing new meaning, purpose, and identity for good or ill, it is a bit astonishing that most psychotherapists and medical professionals haven't recognized their potential for healing. It would be rare indeed for a secular professional such as a psychotherapist or physician to suggest a ritual, especially a religious one, as a part of getting well.

What doesn't seem odd at all is that God sometimes chooses to work powerfully through our human need for rituals that touch our hearts.

Chapter 2

What Are
Personal Healing Liturgies?

Exploring individually created liturgies with individuals and small groups has been a natural outgrowth of my healing ministry of Gestalt Pastoral Care. By turns I have been increasingly surprised, moved, awed, and challenged as I catch glimpses of the power in the church's liturgical treasures, especially when recast to meet one person's life at a particular time. Such liturgies braid together the crucial strands, so often separated both by the church and by psychology, of emotional and spiritual growth.

Burying the Hatchet

Jane had worked hard all her life to erase her own impulses, especially those related to anger. When she finally accomplished the dubious feat of ignoring her interior feelings, her anger did seem to disappear. For a time she felt better and more in control. After a few years, however, she developed frequent headaches so debilitating that they sent her to bed. Her doctor told her that severe muscle tension was the culprit and prescribed muscle relaxers for her. About the same time a friend suggested that perhaps Gestalt Pastoral Care could help as well.

Quickly the root issue surfaced. As a child Jane was subjected to a constant and humiliating verbal barrage. If she protested or got angry for the way she was treated—a natural and healthy reaction—she was severely punished. In her world, anger was not just bad; it was downright dangerous. She learned early that it was much safer to curb her rage and be a good girl. Understandably, anger was still plenty frightening when she became an adult.

Because Jane was terribly afraid of her own anger, she was vulnerable to a commonly skewed attitude among church folk. Even though she knew better, planted into Jane's soul was the idea that Christian love compelled her to stamp out her anger completely. What had been a way of survival as a child had morphed into a distorted way of loving God as an adult. Frankly, I was amazed she had any fire left at all by the time she came to see me.

Jane worked hard, and soon she began to experience some changes. She was less afraid and much more indignant. As we prayed together, it seemed clear that Jesus was *inviting* her to express fully the anger that was, after all, truly inside her. She gradually gave herself permission to express anger, even rage, loudly and physically in a safe place: my office. Using a plastic bat to attack a pillow that stood in for her childhood tormenters, Jane was exhilarated to find strength she didn't know she had. She was astonished to discover that a crucial part of her healing was the expression of long-stuffed anger in a way that hurt no one.

After discovering her angry voice, Jane was a streaking comet. Her tension receded dramatically, and her headaches diminished both in frequency and severity. She discovered a new assertiveness in herself, as well as a delightful and playful wit. She learned to voice her opinions even if they opposed those of a friend. She stood up for herself; she told people off; she brooked no slights; she gave few breaks; she snarled when her toes were stepped on; and she felt wonderful and strong—for a time.

Then the comet fizzled. After some soul-searching, Jane had to admit that her newly acquired short fuse was now poisoning her relationships and making her miserable. She ruefully admitted that she blazed up so often and so intensely that she was in danger of losing some dear friendships. Being an angry woman whom "no one wanted to mess with" had become both a powerful habit and a new identity. What had been a necessary and important stage in her growth was now a constricting trap. Being *afraid* of getting angry had become *having to* get angry.

Then her work shifted. Wisely, she knew she needed to balance the capability of getting angry when appropriate, with the choice to accept, and even love, the foibles of others. She prayed; we prayed and worked hard. Slowly she felt her anger becoming more integrated with the rest of her. She made quite a bit of progress along these lines, but habits stick like lint. Despite her desire to change and her hard work, she was unable to carry herself the whole distance. Occasionally her temper still flared hot over slight insults. Sometimes she took offense when none was intended. Then one day, after beginning her session with prayer, she looked up at me and forcefully declared, "I want to bury the hatchet. It's time."

It seemed to me, too, that the time was ripe, so I suggested we create a liturgy to respond to this new movement of grace. Jane loved the idea. Her comment about burying the hatchet would be our place to begin planning, and we would work out the rest of the details together. Together we decided that she would invite a few friends to be with her while she actually buried a symbolic hatchet.

On the day of Jane's liturgy, four good friends arrived at her house. After I led a call to worship, an opening prayer, and a hymn, Jane read the Gospel story about Jesus insisting that the children not be turned away. Then she told her personal "gospel" story, beginning with her harsh childhood, leading to her pilgrimage from mousiness through assertiveness into bear-trap anger, and finally to her recent longing for real integration. She spoke of how Jesus had accepted and healed her childish anger and fear, and how God was continuing to lead her. She explained about what had gone into the impulse to bury the hatchet at last, and she asked her friends for their response. All expressed how moved they were by her story, and all supported her new resolve. Putting that informal response into liturgical form (which I made up on the spot), each of us in turn then put our hands on Jane's head and said,

> "Jane, I have heard your desire to bury the hatchet. In the name of Christ I support this burial. I will pray for you, and I stand ready to be there for you as you live into a new balance. Amen."

Visibly strengthened by our support, Jane led us to the woods in back of her home, where she had placed a shovel and a special rock she had chosen. About the size of a toaster, the heavy rock would symbolize the hatchet she had been carrying. As Jane began to dig in the hard-packed earth, we stood in a circle around her, singing hymns and praying for her empowerment to truly bury the hatchet. It took her nearly twenty minutes to dig a hole deep enough for such a large rock, but no one rushed her. No one helped her either, for the digging was her hard work to do. We did help her roll the stone into the hole, and someone commented that it reminded her somehow of rolling away the stone of Jesus' tomb. After helping Jane cover the rock with dirt, we laid our hands on her and prayed in thanksgiving for what had occurred, and for Jane's continued healing. The service ended with Eucharist in Jane's house, followed by supper together.

Later Jane struggled to put into words what happened for her that day: "When that rock clunked into the hole in front of everyone, I felt something inside me click into place. I'm sure I forgave those people from my childhood more deeply at that moment than I ever have. I just sort of let go of it. I don't feel anymore that I have to fly off the handle every time someone pushes my buttons. Having my friends there praying has given me strength somehow, and I'm not as hair-trigger now. It's as if a door closed, and I really do feel different. It's wonderful. I haven't popped off at anyone for no reason for weeks, and I haven't had any headaches. But I know that if there was a real reason to use my anger to protect myself or someone else, I could do it."

Jane's hatchet-burying liturgy vividly illustrates the characteristics of individualized Christian liturgies.

First, we didn't plan her liturgy as a quick fix or as a way to avoid the hard work of growth. Jane had worked diligently to grow, and she expected to keep at it. The liturgy did not eliminate Jane's growth process but played an important role in it.

Individualized liturgies usually have the most impact when one is well along in a healing process. Occasionally an individualized liturgy will break up a logjam early on but usually just has the effect of making it possible for the person to do the hard work required for growth. Individualized liturgies of healing seek, on the one hand, to proclaim God's action and desire, and, on the other, to make way for human response.

Jane's liturgy was not a way to crush a part of herself she didn't like, but a way to open the door to new integration. A liturgy of burying the hatchet would have been wildly inappropriate if Jane had not already explored her anger deeply, been willing to express it, and, in a sense, "made friends" with it. Jane had learned both the positive, healthy strength of her anger and also its toxicity, and she was not pining for her old, repressed existence. Rather, Jane wanted to express her anger appropriately from time to time, and she wanted to learn to relate with others gently, tolerantly, and lovingly. By her own account, her special liturgy helped her move toward this new way of living.

We didn't treat the liturgy as magic. We weren't trying to compel God to act for us through arcane words or actions. Most certainly we were not invoking a charm or casting a spell. Instead we were seeking to proclaim Christ's love in a special way, and to cooperate with healing grace. We were not trying to charge Jane's batteries with personal power; rather, we were supporting her surrender to God's healing work.

Furthermore, none of us was under the illusion that this liturgy would simply eradicate Jane's quick temper. Her prayer that day was not made of rigid resolve to never, ever lose her temper again; clearly such resolve would have been unrealistic and unhealthy. Instead her liturgy expressed Jane's desire to grow *toward* a new way of living in which she could depend on grace to teach her how to follow Christ more faithfully. Her experience of a dramatic shift in the weeks after the liturgy gave clear evidence of God's power and grace, but we all knew that this shift would need to be supported by disciplined hard work and the flexibility to cut herself some slack.

Jane's individualized Christian liturgy was not a pep talk. Her liturgy sent no message that Jane should simply snap out of it. It was not a way to inspire Jane into changing, but rather a means of supporting and praying for the change she knew she was called to make.

Jane's liturgy was not coercive or condemning in any way; instead it was respectful and gentle. The thrust was not, "You know better, Jane! How could you have given in to such unchristian behavior? Stop it right now!" Instead we planned the liturgy to carry a message of celebration of the movement of grace in Jane's life, and her desire to align herself with God's continuing invitation to grow.

Further, *the liturgy was done only with Jane's explicit and detailed permission, and the wording and flow came from Jane's own expressed desire, the language of her inner life, and the liturgical wisdom of the church.* She and I planned it together. When I created the congregational response during the service, I asked her if the wording was right before we went ahead.

The little congregation of Jane's friends "worked through" Jane's liturgy together. (After all, the Greek root word for liturgy means "work of the people.") Our plan was carefully made ahead of time but not set in concrete. The informal setting, the good friends, and the very personal nature of the service made it natural for us to be flexible. The small congregation felt free to take an active but limited part in shaping the liturgy. Without changing our general plan, Jane's liturgy was enriched as we made room for small but important additions as we went along. We also were comfortable with Jane's own reactions and were able to respond to her in the context of the liturgy.

So, for example, while we were still in the house, a friend suggested a hymn that she knew Jane loved and, with Jane's permission, led us in singing it as we walked to the woods behind Jane's house. Another pointed out that the large rock Jane had chosen seemed particularly accurate as a symbol of the heavy burden Jane had been carrying, and we took some time to imagine together in silence the impact of its weight on Jane. When we realized that it would take some time for Jane to dig her hole, we sang hymns softly. Jane wept several times during the liturgy, and each time we paused while someone held her until she was finished. When time came for the prayer of confession, Jane decided that instead of praying silently, she wanted to mention aloud some of the hurts she had caused, and to hear words of forgiveness specific to her. Later, over supper, the process continued in an unplanned time of sharing. Spontaneously, the group fell into talking about the power of Jane's liturgy and its impact on each person there.

We did not create a liturgy that would speak only to Jane's mind, for her mind wasn't the problem. Jane knew the changes she wanted to make; she knew it was time to bury the hatchet, but she couldn't do it alone. She had reached the limit of what determination and hard work could accomplish; now she simply needed healing. Thus our liturgy deliberately included some elements that would touch not only her intellect but also her body, emotions, and spirit. The digging in the dirt, the heaviness of the "hatchet," the familiarity of Jane's much-loved woodland setting, the singing of hymns as she worked, the help with rolling the stone, and the celebration of Eucharist in her house, were all important icons that touched Jane on many levels.

I believe the best individualized healing liturgies are designed to ignite every part of our being. Symbolic actions, words of power, involvement of the body, and presence and participation of the church "preach" in a special way, and seem to make pathways in human hearts for God to work. It is no coincidence that back when literacy was rare, the primary method of Christian education was the Mass.

Jane's liturgy, while rooted in tradition, pushed beyond traditional settings and actions. We did not confine ourselves to a church building; in fact a crucial part of the liturgy was the setting: a certain spot in the woods where Jane felt particularly drawn. A shovel and stone are not familiar symbols at Sunday worship but were perfect symbols for God's work in Jane. Burying the stone was not an action that came out of someone else's experience with liturgy, but directly out of Jane's own inner life, and it was specific to her growth journey. However, the flow of our worship that day followed quite closely the United Methodist Holy Communion liturgy, beginning with a call to worship, a hymn of praise, and reading of scripture in Jane's home, then confession and response to the word and a prayer of intercession in the woods. Back in the house, the liturgy culminated with the familiar words of institution, prayer of consecration, and, of course, breaking the bread and sharing the cup together.

Jane's liturgy made room for honest sharing of her inner life and feelings. Jane told her story as it really happened, including how God had healed her so far. As with the sharing that occurs in 12-step groups, Jane made no attempt to sanitize or omit important details.

The framework of the liturgy itself keeps personal liturgies from being simply an emotional display that goes nowhere.

Her telling of her personal story was profoundly honest and accompanied by tears and admission of shame, but we did not set out to create or encourage this intense experience. All we did was listen with loving attention, accepting her feelings as they came.

Usually, intimate sharing is not appropriate in large services of corporate worship. On Sunday morning we may verbally acknowledge that such feelings exist—for example, in a prayer of confession or during the brief sharing of joys and concerns before the prayer of intercession—but ordinarily we keep quiet in church about our in-depth emotional reactions. However, because individual healing liturgies are closely related to pastoral care, it is right to welcome and nurture such expression when it occurs. Just as in a wedding or funeral, tears are not only accepted but expected. The framework of the liturgy itself keeps personal liturgies from being simply an emotional display that goes nowhere. Good pastoral leadership can help keep the balance between allowing time for the release of feelings and maintaining the flow of the service.

Jane's liturgy was held in strict confidence by everyone present. The necessity for confidentiality was made clear when participants were first invited and was underlined when they first arrived at Jane's house. The only person who could talk about what happened there was Jane herself or someone to whom she gave permission.

Although Jane's liturgy focused on one woman's need for healing, worship and prayer—not Jane's journey—were at the heart of the liturgy. We did not dwell on Jane's heroic efforts to change, or on Jane's saintly determination, nor did we let ourselves be titillated by the story of her childhood or the terrible effects of toxic anger. We did not understand ourselves simply as a support group or an audience for Jane's personal saga. Instead, we saw ourselves as church, an ad hoc worshiping community that had come together to pray for Jane in a special way. Our role was similar to that of a parish healing team that goes to a hospital to anoint and pray for someone gravely ill. One person's need shaped our prayers; however, we did not focus on the severity of the need but on receptivity to God's grace. Remember, the ultimate goal of a personal liturgy is not simply to express feelings but to proclaim the gospel in a way that touches a particular person's need for healing. Pastoral leadership is important in helping keep this balance clear.

Although Jane's liturgy grew out of her personal need, she couldn't have prayed this liturgy alone. She needed the church. Even though the ad hoc congregation of close friends was tiny, we clearly represented the larger church. What we did together was confidential and intensely personal but not essentially private. Just like witnesses to a wedding, we were sacred witnesses to Jane's personal story of redemption and growth and her desire to cooperate with grace. We joined her in praise, and together we prayed for continued healing. We marked Jane's important milestone with our presence and support, and we vowed to be with Jane in the future to remind her of the new course she embraced that day. It was vital that we were present as an ad hoc church, for we were church for Jane in the most profound way.

Finally, the small group that gathered for Jane's benefit discovered that Jane was not the only one who received a gift. Jane's friends were moved and intrigued with this new way of being church and were excited and honored to have such an important role in Jane's healing. They wanted to learn more about healing ministry and how laypeople could become involved in it. One woman said that it was wonderful to see for the first time what was involved in ministry, and to be on the giving end of it for once. Some of them had never experienced an intense growth process up close and felt challenged to explore their own growth trajectories. Most found themselves personally touched by grace, and some felt the stirrings of an invitation to grow. At supper they found themselves asking what, for some, were unfamiliar questions: What do I myself need to surrender? to embrace? to admit? to vow? to renounce? Some of them began to imagine having a liturgy of their own in the future; others knew that they were not ready for such vulnerability and commitment.

Some Protestants are rightly suspicious of "empty ritual"—rote repetition because "we've always done it that way." Jane's liturgy was anything but empty. It was full of actions and words that laid bold claim to God's truth. Actions and words of power that were given to us as we asked the Holy Spirit for them. Actions and words of power through which God healed. Actions and words of power that were rooted in the tradition and wisdom of the church, indeed which used familiar Christian liturgies in new ways.

Chapter 3

Opportunities for
Personal Healing Liturgies

Personal healing liturgies are most appropriate when they relate to times of crisis or change in one person's life. Because personalized liturgies are a bridge between pastoral counseling and the corporate life of the church, usually the occasions for personal liturgies are just that: deeply personal and inevitably varied. Personal liturgies can be created to celebrate or mourn, to recognize growth or stagnation, to claim or surrender, to give up false hope or hold fast to the Love that will not let us go. The following are eleven situations that might suggest an opportunity for a personal healing liturgy.

1. When experiencing a life transition or reaching a milestone

In our culture and in the church, we could do much more to celebrate successive life stages and roles. Certainly not everyone who passes a milestone would want a liturgy, but for those who are committed to their faith and serious about continued growth, a liturgical rite of passage can be wonderfully nourishing. Consider these:

- recognizing graduation from high school or college and the new responsibilities ahead

- celebrating retirement from a life of meaningful work, and the new challenge of assuming the role of sage and elder

- embracing the possibilities and limits of becoming a grandparent

- blessing a young person when she begins her first job

- marking liturgically both the betrayal, pain, dashed dreams, and perhaps sin leading to divorce, and the always-present possibility of healing and future happiness

- recommitting to marriage vows after a crisis of relationship has been successfully weathered

I know one couple that holds a private family celebration when each of their daughters menstruates for the first time. Rather than being embarrassed, each daughter looks forward to her special dinner, which includes a liturgy of thanksgiving and a carefully chosen present.

2. When desiring vocational dedication and blessing

We church folks say we believe in the ministry of the laity, that God calls Christians to many different vocations, and that any genuine vocation, whether "sacred" or "secular," is holy. Yet our liturgical actions proclaim just the opposite. Generally the only vocations that we mark liturgically are ones involving direct service to the church. Have you ever experienced—or even heard of—a special church service for someone entering medicine, or social work, or farming or child care, even when she or he is answering a deeply felt and carefully discerned call? For that matter, how often does the church make available to those called to "secular" ministries a system of wise mentors, spiritual directors, and committees that could be called upon to help with vocational discernment? Those who think they may be called to Christian ministry—work in the church institution—have a great deal of support. Those whose Christian vocations are elsewhere have almost none.

A notable exception is found in the deaconess movement in the United Methodist Church. Deaconesses are laywomen who feel called to vocations of love, justice, and service that might not be directly related to the church institution. They engage in such ministries as health care, teaching, social work, community organizing, or human rights. To become United Methodist deaconesses, they must enter into a careful discernment process with their mentors, and pass screening tests and courses in theology, Bible, and mission theology. Periodically they must report in and attend continuing education events. The church formally recognizes their status as deaconesses and gives spiritual—and sometimes financial—support to their various ministries. At this writing there are relatively few United Methodist deaconesses and home missioners (the new, male counterpart of deaconesses) in the United States, although with active recruitment underway, the numbers are in a definite upswing.

I believe that ministers need to develop more ways to recognize liturgically that Christians are most assuredly called to vocations outside the church institution. Why not offer laity the opportunity to dedicate their work to the Lord and receive the blessing and spiritual support of the church and their own personalized liturgy of dedication to their Christian vocation? The services of vocational dedication I have led have meant a great deal, even years later, to the recipients.

3. When inner growth calls for celebration and recognition

People who are in an active growth process can expect to change. Sometimes it seems as though they shed their old skin, almost becoming different people, or perhaps they just become more profoundly themselves. When old habits die, there is more room for other parts of themselves to shine. They give up control and find in themselves new flexibility. They may discover their strength, resiliency, or artistry. They give up singing old dirges and risk living in a new key.

These changes are often apparent to others but are even more obvious to the one who has grown. Sometimes liturgical recognition and celebration of personal growth can help a person embrace a new identity more fully and anchor a new self more firmly as part of God's continuing creation. Someone who has reached a point of integration and new identity can feel the need to take new vows for the living of her life, and to surrender old and destructive patterns to God.

Jack, an Episcopal priest, at a celebration of Eucharist with close friends, added the name Francis (after Francis of Assisi) to his given name. Jack wanted to symbolize the more joyous new man he was becoming after a two-year period of turmoil and rapid inner growth, and he wanted the church to bless his journey and pray for his continued growth. Because he "felt like a new man" and at the same time was "embracing his past in a new way," he felt it especially appropriate to add a new name to his old one.

> *Someone who has reached a point of integration and new identity can feel the need to take new vows for the living of her life, and to surrender old and destructive patterns to God.*
>
> ⤳

Jack wrote some vows for his name-adding service. In the presence of an ad hoc congregation of seven people, he told the story of how God had recently blessed him with much growth and healing. Then he formally took vows in which he promised to love more fully and sacrificially, to pray more faithfully, to exercise his ministry with renewed dedication, and to find times for rest and play. Because he was with good friends, he was able to allow himself to enter deeply into this experience. Jack's tears and trembling voice witnessed to the profound meaning the vows held for him.

After his vows, each of us present stood in front of him in turn, looked into his eyes, and said, "You are now Jack Francis, servant of God. I promise to call you by your new name to remind you of how God has made you new at the age of forty-three. And I promise to support you in the vows you have just taken." Then each of us laid hands on his head and prayed for him. After each prayer, Jack Francis responded that every time he heard his new name, he would remember his promise to live more faithfully and with greater passion.

After we shared Eucharist in his Manhattan apartment, all of us walked to a small bistro in his neighborhood for a late supper. For us the service was still continuing as we talked and ate and laughed together, and it seemed clear that the boundary between sacred and secular had faded away. The little restaurant seemed to shine with holiness and, yes, with eucharistic presence.

Two years after his personal service, Jack Francis was accosted on the street by a mugger who demanded his wallet and then shot him. Jack Francis died instantly. Even as we mourned his senseless death, those of us who had been invited to his name-adding liturgy were able to celebrate his life in a special way. Since the service, he had indeed lived more passionately, more intensely, more lovingly. And in an odd way, we felt that the service prepared him—and us—for his death.

4. When a growth step seems difficult or scary

Sometimes an inner growth process calls for an action or movement that may be not only new but also scary and difficult. Telling a family member that you love him, for example, may feel like jumping off a cliff if your family has never communicated feelings easily. Looking for a new job; learning a new skill; setting aside time for rest, fun, and retreat; going on a mission project for a few weeks; volunteering in a prison; or making an appointment with a doctor or a psychotherapist can all seem like major hurdles to one striving to overcome an inner taboo forbidding such behavior.

When someone sincerely wants to take a certain action and knows that this is his next step, a short personal liturgy of commissioning can immensely support growth. In such a liturgy, the ad hoc church can recognize the difficulty of going ahead, anoint and pray for the person, and then formally send him out in the name of Christ to do what he knows he must. After a service of commissioning, the small congregation continues to support the person's growth by agreeing to ask him about his commissioned task in a few weeks, to keep on praying with him, and to generally offer supportive friendship. With this simple liturgy, laity are naturally brought into pastoral roles, and they continue to care about their friend.

5. When guilt is carried

Most Protestant churches have a prayer of confession as a part of the regular Sunday service. Sometimes, though, one who is carrying guilt for a major sin may need face-to-face confession. He may need to tell the story in all its shameful details to a pastoral listener; the general prayer of confession prayed in unison on Sunday morning just doesn't do it for him. He needs to hear liturgical words of forgiveness with his own name in front of them and made specific to his life. He needs to hear that God still loves him and that there is a way to start over. Anointing is often a natural part of this Christian liturgy and can be a sign of cleansing, of blessing, of starting over, or of healing mercy. This is an instance in which there might be only two persons present: the penitent and the minister, although confessions sometimes seem appropriate in personal liturgies attended by an ad hoc church. For example, "Becoming a Man" on page 103 tells a story of a personal liturgy in which a confession was witnessed by everyone in attendance.

We Protestants have much to learn in this area from Episcopalians and Roman Catholics. As a minister who has practiced hearing confessions for many years, I can say that almost no pastoral activity is quite as rewarding. Watching God at work and seeing long-held burdens slide away with tears of relief and joy is wonderful indeed.

6. When it is time to forgive

Humanly speaking, deep forgiveness of someone who caused profound hurt is nearly impossible. Yet for a Christian, healing from a major hurt is not complete until forgiveness is offered. I am not talking about the pasted-on, smiley, too-fast forgiveness that many church folk confuse with the real thing. Real forgiveness takes time and sweat and usually involves facing the depth of your rage, feeling the extent of your hurt, expressing both (though not necessarily in the presence of the one who hurt you), admitting any way you helped cause the problem, and then eventually surrendering the anger that felt so empowering. Praying to love the person, to see her/him through the eyes of Christ, is often a part of the process too. We have a call to keep working and praying toward forgiveness until it is complete. Thus, genuine forgiveness comes as a result of hard inner work and, most importantly, as a good measure of grace.[1]

When a person of faith is in a difficult forgiveness process, he or she almost certainly will need pastoral help.

Although therapists have recently shown interest in the psychological benefits of forgiveness, the very ones who might help a person get ready to forgive may misunderstand forgiveness. Or they may not believe in forgiveness. Many psychotherapists still think of forgiveness as irrelevant, disempowering, and inherently dishonest. They may imagine that forgiving implies approval of what the other person did, or that one should no longer protect oneself from an abusive or dangerous person. Or they may think that forgiveness is remotely possible only when the offender repents, apologizes, and atones.

When a person of faith is in a difficult forgiveness process, he or she almost certainly will need pastoral help. A personal liturgy of declaring forgiveness *at the appropriate time and after much inner work* can be a great blessing. The person or institution being forgiven is usually present only symbolically. One woman knit a "shawl of forgiveness" for a friend who had badly hurt her. As her ad hoc congregation sang hymns and prayed for her old enemy, she bound off the final stitches. Slowly she folded the completed shawl and placed it on the altar while speaking to her friend as if she were present: "Susan, I have been praying for months with every stitch in this shawl that I would be able to extend to you the forgiveness of Christ. Now, by the grace of God, I can say here in the presence of these witnesses that I do forgive you with my whole heart." Later her ad hoc church anointed Susan, prayed for her continued healing, and shared Eucharist together.

Another person poured a large bucket of muddy water onto the ground as a sign that he was finally ready to let go of the poison of a long-held, hateful grudge. Then, with carefully chosen liturgical words, his friends poured fresh cleansing water over him, water that mingled with his tears of relief and joy. They, too, shared Eucharist and prayer for the man that his healing continue and deepen.

7. When there is need to surrender

Sooner or later, Christian spiritual growth puts you right up against the conflict between your voracious desire to stay in control and your call to surrender more deeply. Not all control is detrimental, of course, but you do need to give up trying to control the uncontrollable and learn to trust that all is in God's hands. Calcified ideas of how things must be in order for you to be happy, notions about exactly what shape your healing must take, attempts to change another person, dearly held prejudices and rigidities, and detailed ideas of how your children must turn out are all examples of control gone amok. So are torpedoing your spouse's wishes and opinions, keeping a tight lid on your feelings, clinging to certain behaviors that hurt others or yourself, orchestrating your life so that you are seldom in a position of vulnerability or inexperience, and trying to control an addiction with your own willpower. Seasoned 12-steppers know well that the first steps in recovery involve admitting powerlessness and surrendering control.

A large proportion of liturgies I have led have been liturgies of surrender. Admitting in the community of faith that it is time to let go of specific ways of trying to control the world is a wonderful way to create inner spaciousness so that something new can be born. Surrender is a prerequisite for living a more faith-filled and trusting life, and most of us need to keep surrendering more and more deeply as we grow. It's as if God says, "Come on. Come on, now. Trust me to take care of things. 'My yoke is easy and my burden is light.'[2] You don't have to carry such big burdens. Give the control back to me."

Most letting-go liturgies involve "physicalizing" the surrender. For example, the surrendering person might actually hold tightly to a symbolic physical object and then perhaps drop, give, or throw it away. One man set down a heavy backpack that he said was the burden of having a spectacular career. During a personal service one woman solemnly laid on the altar a letter in which she resigned from the impossible job of making sure her neurotic parents were always happy. Then she and her ad hoc church prayerfully and lovingly committed her parents to the care of the Lord. Another person, sick and tired of playing the crushing role of family outcast, asked her ad hoc congregation to tie clothesline around her as a visible sign of her cooperation with her own oppression. The rope was then snipped away piece by piece as someone read:

> "The spirit of the Lord is upon me,
>> because he has anointed me
>> to bring good news to the poor.
> He has sent me to proclaim release to the captives
>> and recovery of sight to the blind,
>> to let the oppressed go free,
> to proclaim the year of the Lord's favor." (Luke 4:18-19)

8. When grief prevails

Many pastors work hard to personalize funerals, to reflect both the unique life of the dead person and the particular meaning the death holds for the mourners. The death of an old person is experienced differently from that of a child. The family of someone who dies suddenly in an accident has different needs from the family whose loved one dies after a long, agonizing illness. Caring pastors know that they must find different words of comfort for each situation, and different styles of conducting each funeral. Singing the dead person's favorite hymns, arranging photos or other displays, telling stories that illustrate a certain individual's life are all good additions that can make the traditional service glow with meaning and hope.

Personalized funerals reflecting the nuances of actual life experience are well appreciated by families and friends, and offer help in the long process of saying good-bye. Good personalized funerals engage both the close-knit community of faith and even those who identify with their religion in a minimal way.

Personalized funerals reflecting the nuances of actual life experience are well appreciated by families and friends, and offer help in the long process of saying good-bye.

But what if someone's grief concerns not the loss of a dear one but the loss of a rewarding job or the death of a cherished pet? Ending an important relationship, the death of a dearly held dream, physical impairment, realizing that one's youth is gone forever, or suffering a miscarriage—all of these situations can also be occasions for deep grieving. And what if someone mourns alone, either because of geographic separation, the passage of time, or because others do not share a particular grief? Much wrenching grief is not acknowledged liturgically or culturally, but it is present all the same in various profound losses. Even though there are few specific worship resources for such circumstances, the church still can, and should, respond pastorally and liturgically.

Imagine the impact on a child grieving over the loss of her beloved dog when the pastor or another church member conducts a brief but personalized backyard funeral. A special prayer might be said for the child's healing, including mention of the particular habits of *this* dog: how he snuggled up to his small human friend as she watched TV, how he waited for her all day to come home from school, how he was always ready to play tug-on-the-rope. Perhaps there could also be a ceremonial arranging of a picture of the dog, along with his leash, toys, and bowl, in a prominent place in the child's house as a reminder that nothing can take away good memories.

Or imagine the sadness of an adult who must reluctantly sell family heirlooms and a treasured homeplace. Such a person might greatly appreciate a service of thanksgiving for all the good times, and prayers for healing of the bad ones. Appropriate at such a service would be a moment of formally saying good-bye. It might be important to hold the service at the house, and, as part of the liturgy, walk through the entire house and then shut the front door for the last time.

9. When desolation takes over and hope is fragile

People buffeted with devastating tragedy and catastrophic loss often receive an outpouring of care when their pain is new and sharp. Friends write cards, bring food, call frequently, and make time to help out. But what happens months or years later when the pain may still be debilitating, energy sapping, and faith eroding but is suffered alone out of a desire to not ask any more of a pastor or friends busy with their own concerns?

I believe that a personal liturgy at that point of despair, when the person feels that God has abandoned him and hope is nearly gone, can be powerfully healing. Such a liturgy could begin with recognition of the suffering that is occurring and then focus on an icon of hope that has personal meaning for the sufferer. For example, one woman released dozens of colorful helium balloons as a sign that despite her despair and inability to pray, she chose to believe that God wanted her to be healed and to soar again. Another woman, with some good friends and her spiritual director, planted a "garden of hope" (her story is on page 147); still another lit candles in a pitch-dark cave. Just before each candle was lit, the woman named a "darkness," an aspect of her life that had fallen apart as the result of a devastating crisis. As each candle blazed up, the ad hoc church responded with, "The light shines in the darkness, and the darkness did not overcome it!"(John 1:5). Each of these liturgies included hymns, scripture, confession, anointing, laying on of hands, and a concluding Eucharist. One included foot washing as well.

10. When lies feel like truth

Many of the folks sitting in our pews heard terrible—and false—messages about themselves as children. Well-meaning parents have said such things as:

- "You are such a bother! Just shut up!"
- "You will be the death of me yet."
- "You are a really bad boy/girl."
- "No one will like you if you don't calm down."

I call statements like these lies, because they convey a belief about the child's basic personhood directly opposite to that proclaimed by the gospel. The good news we preach says that no one is a bother to God; that a child's misbehavior does not cause a parent's death; that a child is not inherently bad but cherished by God; and that God loves noisy, active kids as well as calm ones.

Sometimes childhood lies were never articulated but were communicated all the same through the way the child was treated.

- A child whose feelings and needs were often disregarded may learn that his life doesn't matter.

- A child whose loved one abandons him by dying or leaving may conclude that no one, not even God, can be trusted, and that love should be avoided because inevitably it leads to heartache.

- A child who was frequently struck by adults can come to

believe that she deserved such treatment. As an adult she may attack her own children in similar fashion.

• A sexually abused child learns, among other things, that her very personhood is unimportant except to be used for an adult's pleasure.

People continue to learn lies as adults. Someone who is repeatedly passed over for a promotion may conclude that he is a loser. A woman whose husband leaves her for a younger woman may feel that she isn't good enough, especially if she has gained weight or is beginning to show her age. One who is ridiculed repeatedly may begin to feel ridiculous. Adults who are excluded because of race, ethnicity, gender, or lifestyle can begin to believe emotionally, if not rationally, that what others say might actually be true.

Thus terrible admonitions, predictions, and labels carry astonishing power to shape adult lives. Many brave adults have worked hard to dislodge damaging lies and usually do become rationally clear that the lies are, in fact, lies. Even so, the lies may burrow into souls—covert, invasive, and persistent—and the individual finds himself or herself still reacting as if the lies were true.

Lies that attack and erode the personhood of an individual can sometimes be neutralized by the authority of the church to speak the truth. I have developed a simple liturgical practice that I call "Naming Lies, Speaking the Truth." The framework of this personal liturgy, often used in my healing ministry in the context of Eucharist, echoes the Sermon on the Mount, where several times Jesus says, "You have heard that it was said . . . But I say to you . . ." (Matt. 5:21-48). Basically, this liturgical form involves anointing the person before each lie is named, identifying each lie as a lie, and then formally declaring the gospel truth in the name of Christ.

Over the years I have adapted this form to suit many different situations. Ad hoc churches have addressed lies such as, "I have to punish myself." Or, "I can't let myself feel better if my family still feels bad." Or, "I'm not allowed to surpass my father." Or, "If I really let myself get creative, no one will like me, and God will think I'm proud." Again I repeat that liturgies are not magic or therapy, and they cannot be used as a shortcut to avoid deep and truthful inner work. But for those who are ready, "lies and truth" can personalize the gospel in a way that people of faith can assimilate; God enables hearts to embrace what minds already know. Almost always one who is the focus of a "lies and truth" liturgy feels an immediate positive shift.

A guide for "Naming Lies, Speaking the Truth" can be found in the appendix, page 177. I have often used this guide as a framework for introductory workshops on personal healing liturgies. For some adaptations of the "lies and truth" form, see "Good Enough!" on page 125 and "Liturgies in Healing from Sexual Abuse," page 151.

11. When someone has suffered great wounding

Ministers of healing often pray for those who have suffered greatly because of the sins of others. Wrenching traumas can inflict painful wounds that are not easily healed. Although the following list may sound extreme, many ordinary people have experienced such horrors as:

- childhood sexual, physical, or verbal abuse

- domestic violence

- rape

- cataclysmic tragedies

- betrayal by one who was loved and trusted

- abandonment by one who should have been constant

- public humiliation

- stereotyping, victimization, and even violence due to sexism, racism, homophobia, ageism, or classism

From long experience of working with various traumas, I have come to believe that with a commitment to hard work and prayer, even the worst is healable. I don't mean that a deeply wounded person will somehow be able to just go on with life as if the wounding never occurred. Scars can be redeemed and turned into gifts, becoming a source of wisdom, love, and even joy that can be tapped to help others. Again and again I have seen this happen as hurting people experience the healing of Christ. A deeply wounded, profoundly healed person is like a tree that has grown around a boulder; sometimes the tree actually incorporates the boulder into its structure. A boulder tree is especially beautiful and becomes an inspiration to those still struggling to grow around their own obstacles.

When there has been great wounding, personal liturgies can play an important role in a larger healing process that may include psychotherapy, medication, residential treatment, and other intensive means of growth.

For individuals who are deeply wounded, personal liturgies can play an important role in a larger healing process that may include psychotherapy, medication, residential treatment, and other intensive means of growth. When compassionately personalized, familiar liturgical practices can carry a great deal of weight. They can speak directly to a sufferer with the authority of the church and create a new frame around a devastating picture.

Anointing can "preach somatically" about God's desire to touch, cleanse, and bless. One survivor of a physically abusive cult was anointed with many crosses drawn on her face, hands, and feet. As the two-person ad hoc congregation drew each cross, they counteracted the cult's teachings with a declaration, such as: "With this cross we proclaim in the name of Christ that there is no condemnation in Christ." "With this cross we affirm that God has always loved you." "With this cross we remind you that you are connected to Christ, just as a branch is connected to a vine." The survivor found enormous healing in this simple liturgy. The experience became a sort of rudder, a physical and auditory icon to prayerfully recall as she healed.

Foot washing can be a beautiful sign that God wants to touch and heal that which we find most distressing—whatever is painful, wounded, stepped-on, calloused, exhausted, shameful, fearful, or "dirty." It also shows forth the radically transforming nature of God's love, which puts the Lord in the role of slave—or a mother tenderly washing her children. There are social implications here too. Gender, class, and role distinctions are obliterated in this amazing demonstration of God's passionate love. Leading foot-washing services for psychiatric patients, prison inmates, and ordinary retreatants has proven to me many times how deeply this liturgical action touches people of all persuasions and backgrounds. Because foot washing is unfamiliar for most church members, engaging in foot washing can bring the gospel home in a fresh and personal way, especially to those who have suffered greatly.

Eucharist is surely a sign of light shining in the darkness.

Eucharist as a gift of God's presence can convey many levels and nuances of meaning. Eucharist is surely a sign of light shining in the darkness, of Presence, and of Christ given "*for you.*" It reminds us of the church universal and the church triumphant, of inclusion in the family of God, of blessing and brokenness, of divine grace given during a time when the forces of darkness and fear were closing in. A sensitive pastor can make a eucharistic theme come to life with appropriate scripture, hymns, and comments so that the suffering person is addressed personally.

For a short time one woman and I shared Eucharist in my office every week. Each brief, personalized service became an oasis for her as her life was disintegrating. Too demoralized to show her face in church, she said these office eucharistic services "gave her a place to stand," "anchored her in what was really real," and "during all the chaos of that time, they were a resting place."

A natural situation for an individualized healing service occurs in survivors of sexual abuse, who often feel dirty, polluted, and guilty because of what was done to them. Childhood sexual abuse is more common than most people think; experts in the United States say it is rampant. It cuts across racial, social, religious, geographic, and economic lines; boys as well as girls are victims. In most congregations I would expect to find *many* silent and tormented survivors who are too ashamed and pained to share their interior agony with other church members. They may feel that the church could never understand, would blame them for their own abuse, or would even see them as defective.

An individualized liturgy, while not a substitute for the hard work of therapy, can be a powerful experience of God's desire to redeem the all-too-common trauma of sexual abuse. Survivors have reported much healing as they allow the church to minister to them in this way. Busy ministers may feel that work with trauma is best left to the experts and that pastorally they have little to offer in the face of such deep emotional/physical pain. The fact is, the pain of sexual abuse is also experienced spiritually, and the church has unique and vital contributions for abuse survivors, contributions unlikely to be made by secular therapists.

In an individualized liturgy, the church can

- *bless* the created goodness of the survivor's body and cleanse it from emotional/spiritual pollution;

- *declare* in the name and by the authority of Christ that an abused child is not at fault;

- *claim* the survivor's body as a place where the Holy Spirit dwells;

- *demonstrate* that despite what one has been told, everyone has a place around the table of the Lord;

- *shepherd* a survivor through anger to forgiveness. Individualized liturgies are a way for pastors to respond effectively and compassionately while involving a few friends or family in the pastoral care of the survivor, thus validating or creating a natural support system. When planned with care and led with gentleness, such a liturgy can be life-changing and a beautiful supplement to psychotherapy.

The section beginning on page 151 gives examples of different liturgies planned for the healing of sexual abuse.

Chapter 4

Getting Ready to Lead a Personal Healing Liturgy

M uch of the preparation for a personal service of healing takes place long before such a service is suggested. Good personal liturgies for healing depend heavily on the observations, hunches, liturgical experience and expertise, and pastoral leadership of the minister. Before talking about a personal service to a possible recipient, I have found it crucial to think about whether a personal service might be appropriate at this point in the person's growth, evaluate whether the possible recipient and I are ready for it, and formulate a sketchy idea of a possible plan for the service. Actually suggesting the idea of a liturgy or liturgical action and the planning process usually comes later.

Assessing Readiness

1. Decide whether you, the minister, are ready

Because individualized healing liturgies involve more than simply planning and leading a worship service—and because personal liturgies or liturgical actions hold the possibility of both nurturing new green shoots and trampling on them—there are some important personal requirements of the minister. Inevitably, the preparation for a personal liturgy involves sensitive pastoral care, which, of course, continues throughout the flexible service. Frankly, not every pastor has what it takes to lead personal liturgies of healing. Ministers have differing talents and gifts, and some who are inspired preachers, brilliant teachers, or effective administrators and organizers may not do as well with pastoral care. Those who have been trained in pastoral care or spiritual direction, or are involved in healing ministry, or have a natural bent for counseling will be the ones best equipped to help create and lead personal healing liturgies.

> *As with any pastoral care, the minister needs to be relatively free of condemnation and judgments and able to genuinely love the person who will be the focus.*

As with any pastoral care, the minister needs to be relatively free of condemnation and judgments and able to genuinely love the person who will be the focus. Most pastors know, to their chagrin, how quickly their own personal issues can get in the way. A minister who struggles with his own sexual boundaries, for example, may be eager to point the finger at or easily excuse another who is engaging in a similar battle. A minister uncomfortable with her emotions is unlikely to be able to provide the necessary spaciousness for emotional expression in a liturgical context, and may even harbor positive dislike for a person who freely expresses what is inside. A pastor who needs to be in control may not be able to surrender enough to plan a liturgy with one who may be, in his opinion, liturgically or theologically unsophisticated. A minister who has not ventured far from her own tradition or preferences in worship, emotional expression, spiritual language, and personal lifestyle may find it difficult to enter another's inner world as a respectful guest.

This is not to suggest that you need to be a veritable paragon of emotional and spiritual maturity. All of us—pastors and laity—have our weaknesses and our growing edges, and God certainly uses wounded healers. However, if with a particular individual you find yourself judging, controlling, shocked, threatened by another's world, frightened by certain emotions or by emotional depth in general, or unable to allow a style of worship different from your own, your own need for healing or growth probably stands in the way of your ability to love freely. These feelings are a clear signal to step back and let someone else take over.

2. Decide if the person who might become the focus of a personal liturgy is ready

Personal liturgies can be powerful conduits of healing grace, but a wise pastor will not leap to organize liturgies as a universal panacea or just because someone wants one. You must be savvy enough to weed out those who love starring in their personal dysfunctional drama. You would not create a liturgy for someone who wants change but is unwilling to do the hard inner work involved. You would be careful with individuals who are grandiose, severely self-hating, desperate to please, narcissistic, or insisting on support for their personal rigidities—unless they have become aware of what they are doing to themselves, have worked hard to change, and truly long to be healed. Sometimes it makes sense to consult, with appropriate permission, of course, with the person's therapist as you ponder these questions.

Personal healing liturgies aren't for everyone. *Readiness* for a liturgy and *desire* for a liturgy are not the same. Some sufferers might be better served by offering prayer and laying on of hands, pastoral care sessions, or referral to a good psychotherapist.

Before I invite someone to work with me in planning a personal healing liturgy, I look for, in addition to a basic level of emotional and spiritual health, certain other signs of readiness. *Perhaps most important is that the person desiring the liturgy is already engaged in an organic growth process, which may or may not be occurring under church auspices.* Christian retreats, 12-step groups, psychotherapy, pastoral counseling, peer counseling, spiritual direction, programs for physical improvement, or secular workshops are examples of the many ways church folk have found to honor their need to grow. Individualized healing liturgies are a wonderful way to support (not substitute for) such personal-growth work. In fact, a personal liturgy may supply a crucial missing element in a secular growth process because it can honor one's life of faith and point to God's continuing invitation to wholeness.

Mature faith is more able to accept mystery; human inability to control God; and the nuances, unknowns, and rocky paths of holistic growth.

~

Next, the person should have some understanding that her emotional and social growth and her commitment to physical health are vitally connected to her spiritual journey. Ideally she will have a holistic outlook and know that all parts of her interact with one another organically and intimately. If she has not reached that point, I would like to sense that she is at least open to exploring holistic growth.

Third, *the person already possesses a flexible and expectant faith that doesn't prematurely leap to claiming a specific outcome on a particular timetable or cling to a formulaic theology of healing.* Mature faith is more able to accept mystery; human inability to control God; and the nuances, unknowns, and rocky paths of holistic growth. Trust in God's grace—even when God seems momentarily absent or diverted from our deepest desires—is a mark of this maturity. Of course, a suffering person may not be able to easily muster such faith, for suffering itself can make the well of faith run dry. But I would want the person at least to have the inner capacity to assent intellectually, if not emotionally, to the idea that we can't order up the exact kind of healing and growth we want. Instead, we cooperate as best we can and wait for grace to surprise us.

One who is on a conscious and deliberate spiritual journey, or is ripe for taking the first steps on such a journey, is much more likely to benefit from an individualized healing liturgy than one who wants to try a liturgy because she yearns for a cosmic zap that will fix everything.

Further, *I want to be reasonably sure ahead of time that the recipient of a personalized liturgy is strong enough to refuse my suggestions and to voice her own preferences and needs.* Lay folks usually need and welcome pastoral suggestions for liturgy, and even clergy may need a few ideas of possibilities for personalized liturgy they may not have considered. However, if the recipient is too shy to speak up, or so eager to please that her own desires are sacrificed, or too cowed to disagree, the possibility is great that a liturgy intended to focus on her needs will actually be neither personal nor healing. In other words, the liturgy will more likely be tailored for the pastor's own world rather than hers.

An individual is not ready for a personal liturgy until he or she can understand the difference between Christian liturgy and magic rituals. In a personal liturgy we are not conjuring or casting a spell to get what we want. Instead we are seeking to open to God's healing grace.

> *In a personal liturgy we are not conjuring or casting a spell to get what we want. Instead we are seeking to open to God's healing grace.*

One woman, while refusing to go to Alcoholics Anonymous, wanted a liturgy to "get rid of my addiction to alcohol." Another woman wanted a personal liturgy to compel her husband to "love and understand me." A young pastor wanted to have a liturgy to "store up some power so that I can get control of my church board." Furthermore, he wanted God to quiet certain people who were gossiping and sniping behind his back, keeping the church from being a place of prayer, welcome, generous service, and peace. While their motives were worthy, even admirable, these folks did not understand that the function of liturgy is not to control others and certainly not to control God.

A request for a magic ritual provides a natural opening for good spiritual companioning. Quite often these people become willing to surrender their desire to control God once they have had time to get used to the idea. Likely they will still be frightened of giving up control, but eventually they may be ready for a liturgy of surrender.

Finally, *I ask if the possible recipient has some kind of church support system in place, a few close people we could invite to attend the liturgy as witnesses and who would then nourish the recipient's new growth afterward.* Church groups that share intimately—or could do so—such as small prayer or study groups, koinonia prayer partners, and informal groups of good friends, can be natural and wonderful representatives of the larger church in personal liturgies. If the person has no such connections, then we explore ways for the recipient to be supported by good and prayerful church folk who will agree to participate in his liturgy and befriend him afterward. Weekend retreats are a good venue in which to find such support for a personal liturgy. This latter scenario enables both new friendships and the ministry of the laity to bloom. In the process, lay ministers are often challenged themselves to grow in new and courageous ways.

Working on a liturgy together offers a good opportunity to nurture a more mature and grateful faith, greater self-confidence, a deepened experience and theology of church, and a new commitment to grow holistically.

Please keep in mind that these signs of readiness are not set in stone. Every once in a while my discernment tells me to go ahead with a personal healing liturgy even though the recipient does not seem ready according to one or more of these criteria. I am learning that the process of planning and participating in a tailor-made service can be, for some, an arena for *growing toward* these "signs of readiness." Working on a liturgy together offers a good opportunity to nurture a more mature and grateful faith, greater self-confidence, a deepened experience and theology of church, and a new commitment to grow holistically.

Formulating an Informal Proposal

If you feel that both of you are ready, *the next step involves entering more fully into the world of the possible recipient.* You need to discover a bit about the contours of her existence: her inner reality, personal style, worship language, nature of her physical movement, her way of perceiving the world, and her liturgical preferences. This process need not take hours and hours; once you know what to look for, you may be able to quickly form an intuitive impression. So, broaden your attention to the one sitting in your office. You are now actively formulating a loose, informal proposal, so start by putting up all your antennae. Be open to your hunches. Eliminate your personal static as best you can, and tune all your receptors directly toward the possible recipient. Actively seek to form an impression of the person's needs, style, inner language, and physical movement, and let your impression inform a possible focus for a liturgy. As she lets you into her inner world, ask yourself the following questions:

Is there some spiritual companioning to be done before suggesting a personal service?

When a basically mature person expresses a desire to grow in a spiritually misguided or emotionally unhealthy way, he should not automatically be excluded from a personal liturgy. He does, however, need pastoral help in surrendering a dearly held idea of how his healing must occur, and the act of surrender itself could well become the focus of a personal healing liturgy.

Imagine, for example, someone clinging to a hope that her stolid, taciturn, and elderly father will finally tell her that he loves her, and she wants a liturgy to pray that her father will say, "I love you" before he dies. Part of her life has been on hold for years, even decades, waiting for something that probably will never happen. "Ah, but it might," she keeps telling herself, "if only I could just learn to please him." Right there is the trap of false hope that keeps her bound. She believes that the only way she can be healed is through her father's approval; her growth depends on his. Her pain is real, but spiritually she is holding on to an idol. She won't be helped by a liturgy that assails heaven with prayer that her father will finally change.

Some of the most meaningful personal liturgies I have known have not been about joyful movement and growth but have focused on offering some icons of the Holy to hang on to while in despair.

Instead, her pastor might gently ask her if she would be willing to ask the Lord if it is time to surrender false hope in her father's power to heal. Is she willing to ask God to heal her hurting heart in whatever way God wants? In that context, then, with her healing not dependent on her father, she can also pray for him in a new way.

I believe that it is not a pastor's role to tell her she *must* surrender her dream of Daddy's expression of love; instead a pastor or spiritual companion can articulate the question and suggest that she open herself to how God might want to give shape to her genuine growth.

Similarly, if someone is frazzled beyond endurance because he is trying to meet everyone else's needs, he will not be helped by a liturgy that prays for more strength to continue in his unhealthy ways. Instead he might be willing, after some good spiritual companioning and receptive listening prayer, to engage in a liturgy in which he surrenders from trying to save the world.

What might be the focus of the liturgy?

In other words, what special need or circumstance would the liturgy pray for or celebrate? If you have engaged in active spiritual companioning with the person around a particular growth issue, you are probably already pretty clear about the focus. Remember, various personal liturgies can have many diverse goals, even the goal of acknowledging that, though the person is in some kind of desert, God is still present and at work. Some of the most meaningful personal liturgies I have known have not been about joyful movement and growth but have focused on offering some icons of the Holy to hang on to while in despair.

Various personal liturgies can have many diverse goals, even the goal of acknowledging that, though the person is in some kind of desert, God is still present and at work.

I feel that it is important for you, the minister, to articulate, at least in rough form, a possible purpose for a personal liturgy when you finally propose the idea, so that your pastoral leadership is in place from the very beginning. So, for example, I might perceive that with one person I could help plan a liturgy to celebrate a new vocational direction; with another I could help design a service to mourn miscarried babies who died nearly a lifetime ago; and with yet another person I might help her or him design a liturgy of surrender.

How might I anchor the liturgy in the worship traditions of the church? Where do this person's needs intersect with the vast liturgical resources of the church? How does the sweep of the gospel apply to this person's unique situation?

Some of the traditions and practices you may want to consider include the following:

- Eucharist
- scripture and response to the Word
- foot washing
- cleansing or renewal of baptism
- confession and forgiveness
- forgiving
- praise and celebration
- claiming and declaring
- commissioning
- making or renewing vows
- surrendering and renouncing
- blessing and consecration
- anointing
- prayer with laying on of hands (Without this practice, most personal liturgies would feel incomplete.)

Flexibly incorporating Christian sacraments and other liturgical actions helps prevent a personal service from becoming an idiosyncratic exercise in self-involvement, or a secular, but perhaps vaguely spiritual, exercise. When planning longer services, I almost always suggest that Eucharist be the essential context, the bones. Often anointing, confession, foot washing, laying on of hands, and renewal of baptism or marriage vows fit in naturally as well.

Later, when planning with the recipient, I find it important to ask her what Christian worship traditions are particularly meaningful to her. And even though certain practices I suggest might be new to her, I want them to fit her inner style. In other words, I try hard to use the emotional and spiritual "language" of the person who will be the focus of the service. Practices such as making the sign of the cross, praying while standing with arms extended, walking in procession from one place to another, swaying, dancing, bowing, prostrating oneself, using praise music or traditional hymns, classical music, or Gregorian chant have all been important in various personal liturgies I have led. Some of these practices have stretched both me and other participants, but I try to remember that my own preferences and style of prayer do not contain all the truth. Leading these liturgies, I myself have been profoundly challenged and taught.

Once, during a healing workshop, I led a brief liturgical action for a Greek Orthodox woman that featured kissing one another's toes. The largely mainstream Protestant group had to admit that the very idea of toe kissing sounded, well, weird. They were helped by the woman's explanation that in the Orthodox tradition, kissing someone's toe, particularly in monastic circles, does not imply difference in rank or subservience and certainly not worship of a person. Instead, kissing another's toe is really about seeing the holiness of God everywhere. Either barefoot or shod, it is a gesture of deep respect and trust, and is usually reciprocated. Mutual toe kissing, she told us, says that the Christ in me recognizes the Christ in you. Put that way, the workshop group had no trouble agreeing to "act Orthodox" for half an hour. In other words, instead of asking her to adapt to our preferences, we joined her world as best we could. For the Orthodox woman, who had grown up in the only Orthodox family in her small town, sharing this brief liturgical action was an important and healing moment. The experience seemed to overshadow her painful childhood memories as a strange and lonely misfit, and fed her soul with the startling knowledge that she had something of value to teach others, something they might appreciate or even come to treasure.

What are the language preferences of the person who is the focus of the special liturgy? How can I incorporate them?

Countless people, including me, find it difficult to worship if all mention of God is cast in masculine pronouns, and humanity is routinely called "mankind" or "man." If you were leading a liturgy for me, I would emphatically insist that you find ways to refer to God and humanity that are not exclusively masculine. However, I know that others find comfort in the familiar male pronouns during worship. If I were leading a tailor-made service for such a person, it would be incumbent on me *pastorally* to put aside my feminist preferences for the moment and use the other person's language. (In a teaching venue, however, I might try hard to convince the same individual of the need for gender language inclusivity!) Similarly, a young Quaker told a workshop group that when she prayed or engaged in intimate conversation, she liked to use the old Quaker speech, "thee, thy, and thou." It meant a great deal to her when we agreed to use these words as we prayed for her. In a large service such conflicting concerns can't be easily addressed, but for good pastoral reasons I believe in a personal healing service we can and should adapt.

Whether you are suggesting a brief liturgical action or a longer service, you are not imposing a plan, but proposing an idea that almost certainly will be altered as you talk it over with the recipient.

❧

What is the individual's style?

Do you sense that she is shy and retiring, or bold and assertive? Is he a lover of silence, or one who worships best with enthusiastic singing and shouting? Does she seem plainspoken, or dramatic? Does she greet the world from her intellect, or is she more of a hands-on or intuitive person? Is she athletic, or sedentary? Might he respond best to a liturgy that is carefully worded and planned, or one that makes room for a little spontaneity? Is his manner simple and folksy, or formal and ornate?

Remember, answering these questions becomes easier and happens faster as you become more adept at keeping them in mind. You might come to have an intuitive feel or a prayerful discernment about how to match liturgical events to a person's inner style. Whether you are suggesting a brief liturgical action or a longer service, you are not imposing a plan, but proposing an idea that almost certainly will be altered as you talk it over with the recipient.

What is the individual's preferred perceptual modality?

A preferred perceptual modality is the way a person likes to take in information about the world. Here are the four basic perceptual modalities:

- visual (seeing)

- auditory (hearing)

- sensate (physical sensations and intuitive sensing)

- cognitive (thinking, organizing data)

Most people naturally prefer one modality over the other three, and if asked which modality they use when learning or when praying, they can answer quite easily. A simple way to discover a preferred perceptual modality is to ask someone what she notices about the room. Or, ask someone to recall the couch in his childhood house, and listen carefully to how he describes it. Does he say,

- "Our couch was red with little flecks of brown, and it had a crocheted afghan draped over the back" (a visual experience)?

- "Every time I sat on the couch, the springs made a squeaky sound" (an auditory perception)?

- "That couch was really scratchy, but when I wrapped up in the cozy afghan, no matter what was going on in the house, everything just felt okay" (a sensate expression)?

- "For me our couch was a symbol of the best communication in our family, because when we had something important to say, we always sat there" (a cognitive statement)?

It is important to note that most people routinely combine two or more modalities and are capable, in some measure, of all four. Once a pastor gets accustomed to being alert for perceptual preferences, she can often infer what sort of perceiver is talking just from paying careful attention to how he describes his world.

When you know the perceptual preference of the person for whom the liturgy will be organized, you can make sure that at least some important components of the liturgy will match his or her preference. With a visualizer, it is important to pay special attention to colors and shapes, and to employ many visual symbols. An empty bowl, shattered pottery, muddy water, handwoven fabric, a broken branch, a profusion of flowers, and an unusual cross made of nails are examples of icons that have been important for assorted visualizers. For an auditory person, decisions about music may be paramount. Consider also such actions as ringing a gong, listening to the birds, shouting a psalm, sitting in silence, or deliberately breaking the eucharistic bread with a loud snap. A sensate person really needs physical experiences; suggestions for involvement of the body occur throughout this book. Only a very few people are truly cognitive, and it is easy to include cognitive experiences in a liturgy. In fact, if it weren't for the hymns and stained glass, many traditional Protestant liturgies would invite cognitive responses almost exclusively. Ideas are conveyed in spoken litanies and other prayers, in preaching, and most of all, in creedal statements. Even some newly created liturgies are mostly words, truthful words, poetic words maybe, vernacular words sometimes, but still words.

> *When you know the perceptual preference of the person for whom the liturgy will be organized, you can make sure that at least some of the important components of the liturgy will match the way he or she perceives.*

I believe that it is important, insofar as possible, to create liturgies that call forth all four ways of perceiving, with an accent on the perceptual modality of the recipient. Many of the components of the liturgies described in this book invite all four perceptual modalities at once. For example, various members of the ad hoc church that gathered around Jane as she buried the hatchet (see page 33) described deeply meaningful experiences involving sight, sound, sensation, and ideas during the liturgy.

Chapter 5

Leading a
Personal Healing Liturgy

By now you have assessed your own readiness to lead a personal liturgy, and the readiness of the possible recipient. You have decided what issue the service might focus on, and considered liturgical resources that may be appropriate. You have noted language preferences and personal style. Likely you have engaged in spiritual direction as well.

One more preparatory step remains before you share your idea for a personal healing liturgy: planning a way to involve the recipient's body. Most pastors find that this step holds the most challenge for them; it is the longest stretch from what they already know. Somatic involvement is well worth stretching for. Those who have been recipients of a personal healing liturgy usually say that their bodily participation was both vital and memorable.

When well-tailored physical expressions are included in liturgy, awareness blooms and discoveries are made that go beyond thoughts and words. It is not unusual for a person to have a *somatic* experience of grace, offering a fresh and powerful opening for the gospel to take root. Involving bodies, both in traditional ways (such as kneeling for prayer) and in ways unique to a person's particular physical expressiveness (such as Jane's liturgy of burying the hatchet), is a fundamental part of personal services of healing. To be truly personal, we must be holistic!

Here is the heart of it: moving physically can help a person move emotionally and spiritually, especially if that physical movement emerges out of what the person's body already wants to do. Motion, emotion, and devotion are closely intertwined.

Perhaps this idea of unique movement or actions—in worship, no less—sounds a bit over-the-top to you. You may worry that people will feel self-conscious or will simply refuse outright. Admittedly, incorporating physicality in worship may challenge everyone a little, especially those unaccustomed to the idea. Keep in mind that physical actions don't have to veer off into something that seems odd or crazy to the recipient. If he is afraid of anything too different, he might be willing to try such simple actions as holding on to a cross, lighting a candle, walking from one spot to another, opening his arms as a gesture of acceptance, or turning around as a sign of turning toward something new. Remember, too, that if the service is well fitting and truly personalized, even physical actions not usually encountered in worship will, in the end, feel natural.

Motion, emotion, and devotion are closely intertwined.

How to Come Up with Physical Actions

"So," you may ask, "how do I decide what to suggest? How do I know that a particular physical action will fit?" The first thing to keep in mind is that you are making a suggestion, not giving an order. Take into account everything you've observed (including the recipient's physical capabilities!), make your best guess, and allow the recipient to modify the suggestion as you talk together. Be ready to jettison your idea completely and perhaps come up with another one. Always remember: personal liturgies are planned *together*.

Once you accept the idea that all parts of humans are interconnected—body, mind, spirit, emotions, and sociability—making a suggestion for a physical action is not all that difficult. Following are several methods for deciding what to suggest.

1. Pay close attention to metaphors.

People will often tell you what they need to do, if you listen well to the metaphors they use when describing themselves. The English language offers a huge array of physical metaphors to describe emotional and spiritual states. Figure out an easy physical way to act out a metaphor, and you have a suggestion that is quite possibly right-on. (The idea is not necessarily to duplicate the metaphor literally but to suggest ways to explore its meaning somatically.) Many of the physical actions described in this book were created in this simple way. For example, imagine that someone tells you:

- *"I need to break out."* You could suggest breaking a symbolic object: a coconut, a piñata, an egg, or a crockery dish. Or maybe tearing through a large paper bag would be a better fit. Unlocking a door and striding through with some forceful or liturgical words may be right for someone else. Another person might even be willing to "break out" of a tight circle of people or a large cardboard box.

- *"I need to cut the cord."* You might need clothesline and scissors. Or the person might simply make cutting or chopping motions with his hands.

- *"I'm going around in circles."* You could suggest that walking in circles could be part of the liturgy, as well as some well-chosen biblical words or liturgical music that could serve as a signal to stop circling and go straight toward a symbolic object. This "dance" could be repeated several times.

- *"I'm carrying a big load on my shoulders."* What might physicalize the load? A bag of playground sand? Shoulder bags full of something heavy? Pillowcases stuffed with laundry? Pressure from a volunteer's hands? With what liturgical movement, words, or music could the load be put down?

Now imagine how you might make physical actions (perhaps with liturgical responses) out of the following metaphors:

- *"I'd like to get my head out of the sand."*
- *"I need to just drop it."*
- *"I've got to get this off my chest."*
- *"It's time to get rid of all this baggage I've been carrying around."*
- *"I think it's finally time for me to fly."*
- *"I'm in the desert."*
- *"It's been such an uphill climb."*
- *"I'm reaching for God."*
- *"I've been pushing . . . holding on . . . holding in . . . keeping out."*
- *"Everything around me is dark."*
- *"I'm so stuck."*

2. Let the theme of the liturgy shape some suggestions.

Sometimes just sharing with the recipient a few possibilities can spark an idea for a personal action that fits. For example,

- *Liturgies of celebration* could include flying kites; scattering bird-seed or confetti; releasing balloons; singing with gestures; or whirling with long paper streamers, scarves, or pieces of silk.

- *Liturgies of vocational blessing* might involve use of the "tools of the trade." A medical professional might listen with a stethoscope to everyone's heartbeat as the ad hoc church sings softly. A teacher might walk around with his lesson plan notebook, asking each person to touch and bless it. A farmer might arrange and then offer a tray of food she grew, speaking words such as, "I want to cooperate with God to grow this food so you can eat."

- *Liturgies of surrender* could involve tossing rocks into a pond, floating in a pool, falling backwards into the collective arms of the ad hoc church, breathing out that which needs to be surrendered while breathing in a welcome to grace, or prostrating oneself. Other suggestions are leaning on someone who agrees to represent the body of Christ for a moment, or giving that person a symbolic object, putting a symbolic object on the altar, or laying down a burden.

- *Liturgies that mark life transitions* could involve ringing the church bell or a small gong, walking from one symbolic location to another, reaching, stretching, or putting on new, symbolic clothes.

- *Liturgies that recognize desolation and offer hope* could employ hiking up a mountain, shouting a lament psalm, baking bread, wrapping someone in a comforting blanket, unwrapping someone from a constricting blanket, lighting candles in the darkness, or building a bonfire.

3. Point out, or exaggerate a bit, the physicality already inherent in the liturgical traditions of the church.

Foot washing is a prime example of a beautiful physical liturgy. So is anointing with oil; why not also anoint feet and hands as well as the forehead? Or using water, sprinkled or poured, to cleanse, bless, or reaffirm baptismal vows? What about using real bread broken into larger-than-usual chunks at Eucharist instead of tiny wafers or cubes? Or incorporating liturgical gestures, even if they seem a bit new to the recipient, such as bowing, crossing oneself, raising one's arms in praise, or embracing a cross?

4. Ask the recipient what she or he might like to do.

Most people need some suggestions first to prime the pump, but a few can come up with creative ideas on their own, especially if they have had prior experience with personal healing liturgies. One woman, when asked, said that in her liturgy she would like to "dance the new dance I'm being called to dance. I have to move in a way I can't plan for ahead of time."

Upon approaching his dreaded sixty-fifth birthday, a man decided that he needed "to erase the big divide between being sixty-four and being sixty-five." He formulated and carried out a brief liturgical action for himself. He invited two members of his prayer group to his house, explaining that he wanted them to witness a liturgical action. When they arrived on a hot summer day, he made a chalk line on his driveway. On one side he wrote "64"; on the other he wrote "65." Straddling the line, he said: "I want to affirm that when my birthday comes, I will still be the same person I've always been. No matter what age I am, my life is in God's hands, and I will never retire from some kind of ministry. I thank God for every day of my life so far, and for every day I have left. Here and now I'm gonna erase the line!"

He then turned the garden hose on full blast, quickly obliterating the line and the numbers. Laughing with glee, he sprayed his ad hoc church too. Soaking wet, they prayed for their friend, including giving thanks that he was still part mischievous boy.

Proposing a Personal Healing Liturgy

Finally it is time to mention the idea of a healing liturgy to the person with whom you have been working, along with your tentative proposal. Obviously you will tailor your words as carefully as you have tailored your suggestion. Here are some examples.

Suppose you have been considering a personal liturgy for a young man who lives under the pall of mild depression. He has told you that in therapy he has discovered that part of him actually holds on to depression because depression is familiar and safe. At this point in his process, being a depressed person is like playing a role. Change is scary. He just can't imagine who he'd be or what challenges he'd have to meet if he weren't, as he says, "in the pits."

On the other hand, he has told you that he would like to really dive into his life. An emerging healthy part of him is really tired of languishing and wants to get on with things. In some ways he feels eager, even vigorous. But as soon as he imagines actually being different, anxiety hits him in the face. He has been stuck at this point for months.[1] He has tried to pray his way out, but God seems uncaring and faraway.

In proposing a general idea for a personal healing liturgy, you might say:

I have an idea for how some of us could pray for you. Is it okay if I tell you about it?" (You are already sending the message that his permission is crucial.)

Sometimes people who feel stuck are helped by liturgies in which a small group prays for one person. What I'm thinking is that you and I, and a few people you might invite, could go to that deep ravine outside of town, where we would actually join you 'in the pits.' If you think it's a good idea, we could have Communion there, as a sign that God is with you even in your depression. How does that sound to you?" (You are asking for his input from the very beginning.)

Then I'm imagining that you would climb out slowly, remembering what holds you back and what pushes you on. You could take your time, and we would walk with you. You and I could probably think of some liturgical way to address your anxiety and invite God to touch you when we get to the top. One simple thing we could do is gather around you and pray that you learn to trust God more deeply, and that God will show you how to embrace life without depression.

If you want, we could anoint you too, to receive a new way of living that God might give you. We could even wash your feet. Or we could create a completely different liturgy. It's your call. I would want it to be something that feels right to you." (You have laid out a plan with some options. You have also made it clear that the whole plan could be modified or even tossed out.)

Does any of this seem like something you might want to try?

For a more reserved, formal, perhaps older person, also mildly depressed, you might put it this way:

> I know you are feeling really bad these days and wondering if God has abandoned you. This is a really hard time for you, but you don't have to go through this alone, you know. The prayer of a group sometimes helps people who are having a hard time. I wonder if you might let me and maybe one or two others have a special time of prayer for you?
>
> What I have in mind is a brief service of Communion together here in your house or in the church, and then we could pray in a general way for your depression. If you agree, you and I could pick out some hymns or passages of scripture that have been important to you in the past, ones that bring a promise of God's desire to be with you in everything. We might even think about lighting candles as we go along to symbolize the light of Christ with you, even when everything seems dark.
>
> Do you think you might give us permission to do this?

If the person says no to your proposal, back down fast.

Personal healing liturgies should never become a "should." They are never coercive or condemning. You might say:

> I'll be glad to try to come up with a new idea if you would like to do something else, or maybe we could figure it out together; after all, it would be your service. But I really do understand if the whole notion is just not right for you. Personal liturgies don't appeal to everyone. Just thought I'd ask, because some other people have found a personal liturgy helpful, and it played an important role in their healing. If you ever change your mind, just let me know.

If the person agrees to the idea of a personal healing service, think together how to shape the liturgy and personalize it even further.

Be ready to have your idea adapted or even radically changed. Remember that you are the expert on worship, but the recipient is the expert on himself or herself. Continue to listen carefully and stretch as much as possible to put yourself at the service of the recipient. Ask what part of your proposal feels right, and what doesn't. Inquire if there are special hymns or scripture he might like, or if there is an object or action that has personal meaning that might be included. One woman, for example, wanted to use her grandmother's trunk as a eucharistic table. I had proposed to her that we have Eucharist with a few of her friends, followed by the renewal of her baptism. She liked the idea, but she wanted, literally and specifically, to honor her grandmother's Christian teaching as her "foundation." It was a simple matter to do as she asked. In another instance, a man asked if we could somehow incorporate a particular seashell he cherished. He had found the ordinary-looking shell, somehow shining with God's presence, during a time of great fear and uncertainty. For years it had been a special and personal icon of Presence, and now he wanted to celebrate how gently he had been shepherded and how deeply he had been healed. He also asked that we sing the spiritual that begins, "We've come this far by faith / leanin' on the Lord."

A recipient may have some ideas about how to involve his or her body that are quite different from those presented in your proposal. Listen carefully and adapt.

A recipient may have some ideas about how to involve his or her body that are quite different from those presented in your proposal. Listen carefully and adapt, still working back and forth with the person. If he says, for example, "I don't want to go to that ravine! The ravine has been a lover's lane for years, and that's just not what my depression is about," you could respond, "Okay, I get it. How would you like another outdoor location or maybe even a dark basement instead? Or do you have another place in mind?"

Decide where to hold your service.

The setting may become apparent once you decide how the person's body might be involved. Of course, the setting could be in a church or retreat center, but just as appropriate might be a living room or kitchen, a store, a river or pond or ocean, a mountaintop, a waterfall, the woods, a park, a cemetery, a cave, a gully, a garden, a backyard, a playground, a factory, an office, a studio or other place of work, a scene of former trauma, a place of darkness—almost anywhere that takes on personal meaning for the focal person.

Set the date and time.

Anniversaries of important events have been crucial for some. Meeting at dawn, noon, or dusk has held significance for others. For most, the date and time are of no real consequence, and the deciding factor is when you can best coordinate your calendars.

If the liturgy will be long and include many components, it is important to find a time when participants can give several hours without needing to rush off before the liturgy is finished. Adding a simple meal afterward takes even more time but affords the opportunity to talk about what will be, for most, a new experience. These informal conversations afterward often segue easily and naturally into rich and intimate "soul sharing."

Decide whom to invite.

My advice is to keep it small, five or six persons at most. Ask the recipient whom she depends on for support. As pastor, you might also suggest others who could enter into this ministry. I believe it is important that the proposed invitees are already people of faith and have at least some familiarity with healing prayer. In my opinion it is not really important whether they are members of the recipient's church; members of other Christian denominations can greatly enrich a personal liturgy. The idea is to find those who can be active, wholehearted, and prayerful participants in the liturgy, and offer support and friendship afterward.

Occasionally a recipient has a good friend who has no connection to any church. Although I try to consider each instance separately, most often we decide not to invite a person who would require lengthy explanations in order to be a compassionate observer. After all, we would not invite such a person to join a healing prayer team before he or she is even introduced to Christianity. I would, however, encourage the recipient to share with the unchurched friend later what happened at the liturgy.

Leading the Liturgy: Orientation

Even when the participants in a personal healing liturgy are experienced in healing prayer, most likely they will still need a bit of orientation as they gather for the service. I usually explain to the group what a personal service entails, and the recipient and I share briefly the general plan for the liturgy. Knowing what to expect helps participants to enter more fully into a new way of "being church" for a friend. I explain that we will go slowly to give the recipient time to take in what is happening, and I underline the important role they will have as witnesses, intercessors, and supporters. I also explain that although we might make some small changes and additions as we go along, we will do nothing without first asking permission of the recipient. I invite them to feel free to gently break in if they feel moved to lead us in singing, quote scripture, or make a comment, but to make sure that it's okay with their friend. Even if they are on easy hugging terms with their friend, during the liturgy they need to ask their friend's permission for any kind of touch. All of us are

Knowing what to expect helps participants to enter more fully into a new way of "being church" for a friend.

"gathered together" at the service of the one for whom the liturgy is being held, and he or she has the final say. "Remember," I remind them, "we are praying *with and for* our friend, not doing something *to* our friend. We are joining together in worship and prayer, not trying to make something happen or pressuring for change. As best we can, we will trust God to do the work."

I also tell them that although we are gathered to pray for our friend, the service might offer gifts of personal healing or insight to the pray-ers as well. I suggest that they stay aware of their own reactions, and I promise that there will be time to talk after the service is over. I then field questions and generally try to set the tone of informality and reverence. Finally, together we make a promise of confidentiality, agreeing that unless we have explicit permission from the recipient, we will share nothing about her personal story with anyone. We can share our own experience in very general terms. This first part of the orientation with the ad hoc church takes perhaps ten minutes.

Good friends usually already know something of the circumstances that prompted the liturgy. Even so, it is important for the recipient to have the opportunity to tell the whole story—or at least as much as he or she wants to tell at this time. This storytelling is both the second part of the orientation and a natural lead-in to the service itself. Often the story is told with beautiful and terrible honesty, bringing to light that which has been hidden or suffered in secret. Having the gathered church receive the story with tenderness and compassion is often healing in itself.

Leading the Liturgy: Flexibility Is Key

Whether the service is a brief liturgical action or a much longer service, it is important to be flexible, attentive to the pace and process, and open to new material or movements that might be spontaneously woven into the general plan. In a personal service the pastor will need to find a way to lead the group to be open to the Holy Spirit without letting things disintegrate into whims or confusion. Having a traditional liturgical context such as Eucharist to which small additions can be made is a good way to ensure that the liturgy will stay on track.

I find that most of the new material that surfaces during a personal liturgy comes from the recipient herself as she pays attention to her ever-changing inner process. The recipient is literally given room to breathe, with easy silences in which to digest slowly what is happening, and to sense the next step. Frequently throughout the liturgy I ask such questions as, "What's happening with you now?" or "What are you aware of?" or "Are you ready for us to go on?" Since the person enters into a healing process in a personal liturgy, it is crucial to keep checking in and devising simple ways to respond liturgically and sensitively to God's work in the continually unfolding process.

When asked what was happening at a particular moment in her personal liturgy, a woman replied, "I feel a little lighter, as if God's hand is on my shoulder." I asked whether she was willing to say those words to each person, one at a time, and let each respond with, "Alleluia!" She agreed, and this small addition became a sort of touchstone that gave her hope as we went along, that God was indeed at work.

Another person said at one point in his liturgy, "I'm feeling a bit scared all of a sudden." I invited him to say that as a prayer and wait for God's response. He agreed, and the group paused in silence until he was finished, when he said, "God seems to be telling me that God is shaping my future and will be with me in it." I invited him to breathe these words into his body and breathe out his anxiety. Again we waited until he was ready to continue.

Once someone said in the middle of her liturgy, "My goodness. I feel like I'm lying down in the green pastures of Psalm 23." I invited her to lie down on the rug and take all the time she needed to let herself be in green pastures with the Lord as her shepherd. At her request, the ad hoc church sang softly one of her favorite hymns, "He Leadeth Me: O Blessed Thought." Then together we recited the familiar Twenty-third Psalm.

A lonely man who had felt separated from nearly everyone in his life commented during his liturgy, "It's dawning on me right now that maybe I really am part of the church. Even if I don't belong anywhere else, I belong here. I've always known it, of course, but I think shame kept me from really believing it." He asked the ad hoc church to hold hands and form a circle with him, which, of course, they were happy to do. The minister then suggested that each person say to the man, "In the name of Jesus Christ, I affirm that you are a part of the body of Christ." After each statement, the ad hoc church responded, "Amen!"

Responsiveness of the ad hoc church to God's healing process during a personal liturgy is an important part of what makes the liturgy truly personal.

Responsiveness of the ad hoc church to God's healing process during a personal liturgy is an important part of what makes the liturgy truly personal. Helping the recipient become more aware of his inner process is what makes a healing liturgy truly healing.

Leading the Liturgy: Sharing Afterward

Participants at a personal liturgy usually have plenty to say when the service is over. Often they have been moved to tears, challenged to grow themselves, deeply honored to be present at such an intimate occasion, put in touch with their own need for healing, given an experience of God's presence and power, or shown a way of ministry that is most likely quite new. Such profoundly sacred experiences frequently are followed by a natural period of silence as people search for words. But if, after a few minutes, a pastor explicitly invites the participants to share with the recipient what happened for them, they are usually eager to do so.

I structure their responses by saying something like, "Let's share with Anne what happened for us during her liturgy. Now is not the time for questions or advice or preaching or analysis. For now, let's just tell Anne about our own experience—our impressions, what we prayed, what images or words were present to us, how we personally identified with this liturgy, and so on."

I do it this way for several reasons:

- To one who has just allowed herself to be vulnerable, preaching, analysis, or advice can feel like rejection, manipulation, or pressure to change. "I believe . . ." or "I experienced . . ." feels very different from "You should . . ." or "Here's what all this means."

- Simply relating experiences (rather than analyzing or preaching) after a liturgy can model a nonjudgmental ministry of presence for the participants.

- Sharing reactions opens the way for everyone to join Anne in feeling vulnerable. She is less likely to come away feeling that she is the only needy one.

- Anne gets to experience firsthand how revealing her need has blessed her friends.

- Sharing our experiences helps us see how God has worked with everyone present.

- Telling experiences after a personal healing liturgy helps everyone present see how God has worked with the whole ad hoc church, and often opens doors of spiritual growth for the intercessors.

When the sharing is begun in this way, it often continues informally in the same vein as the group adjourns for a meal. The group falls into telling their own stories, sharing doubts and faith, failures and joys. There is also much laughter, horsing around, celebration and hoopla, as well as the exchange of e-mail addresses and phone numbers. Individuals who arrived knowing only the person who invited them now become eager to minister to one another. It is beautiful to watch as new friendships are formed and natural support networks spread out.

A week or so later I generally call or send a brief e-mail to find out how the person who was the focus of our prayers is coming along. Usually I find that the ad hoc church is way ahead of me. They have already e-mailed, called, prayed daily, or even met for lunch, and generally been there for their friend and one another. The initiative of the minister, the willingness and vulnerability of the recipient, and especially the faithful presence of the ad hoc church has begun a spirit-filled process that, once again, has radiated outward among God's people.

Stories
of Personal Healing Liturgies

In the following pages I tell the stories of twenty-three personal healing liturgies. Remember, creating personal liturgies requires that the minister not only plan and lead a service but also take into close account the recipient's story and her preferences in language, worship, and style. In addition, the minister must be as alive as possible to the process of healing that occurs during the liturgy, and sometimes find ways to respond liturgically on the spot to these changes. Leading personal liturgies also calls a minister to be profoundly respectful of the recipient, asking permission for every addition along the way, as well as helping the ad hoc church enter into an experience that may be new to them.

For these reasons, I have told in some detail the backstory that sparked each liturgy, in addition to how the liturgy was planned, what happened during the liturgy itself, and often some of the reactions from the ad hoc church. Because of the fluid and individualized nature of personal liturgies, I have not included any orders of worship here. I have, however, tried to convey the general flow of each liturgy in the hope that others will be encouraged to explore this ministry.

Liturgies of Celebration

Finding Roots

A young Japanese couple immigrated to the United States just before their baby was born. Wanting to fit into American culture, they gave their new daughter the most American name they could think of: Mary Elizabeth. Although they spoke Japanese at home, they strove hard to embrace all things American, including language, customs, clothing, food, and music. By the time Mary Elizabeth went to school, the parents had softened a bit with their self-imposed taboo against Japanese culture and had begun to share the richness of Japanese life with their daughter.

What interested Mary Elizabeth most were the pictures of her Japanese relatives. Grandmothers and grandfathers she had never met. Cousins she had never played with. Aunts and uncles, lots of them. Poring over their pictures, she learned their names and where they lived and what they did. Even as a young child Mary Elizabeth yearned to go to Japan and meet the rest of her family. Her parents wanted to take her, but the airfare was always more than their budget would allow.

Fast-forward to Mary Elizabeth at age thirty-two. She has a good job in New York and has saved enough money to go to Japan and to take her mother with her. (Her father had died five years earlier.) It is literally the trip of a lifetime, a dream come true. She and her mother are welcomed by the whole clan, specially gathered at the family homestead for an unprecedented week of family reunion. There are sumptuous feasts, much storytelling, picture taking, prayers, bowing to show respect, laughter, and tears all around.

In Japan Mary Elizabeth feels she has found a missing part of herself. In an odd and surprising way, she has come home. She is also astonished to discover that almost instantly she loves these people she has never met and that they feel the same about her. Affectionately they give Mary Elizabeth a Japanese nickname, Mariko, which means "child of truth." Mary Elizabeth is delighted. During this wonderful trip it is as if some inner jigsaw pieces fit together for the first time, and Mary Elizabeth feels more integrated and whole than ever before.

Upon returning home to New York, Mary Elizabeth knew she wanted to find a way to share and celebrate her visit to Japan with a few dear friends. As she said, she needed to "bring her Japanese experience home." At her pastor's suggestion, together they created a liturgy they called "A Celebration of Meeting My Family."

Mary Elizabeth's celebration was held in the comfortable, home-like fellowship room of her church. Four close friends were present, in addition to Mary Elizabeth and her pastor. The evening began with Mary Elizabeth sharing at some length about the beautiful welcome she received in Japan, her joy at finally meeting the rest of her family and the instant connection with them, and the inner changes that had occurred as a result.

Enlarged photos of Mary Elizabeth's new family had been placed around the spacious room. After a hymn ("In Christ There Is No East or West") and a prayer, the ad hoc church moved to each picture as Mary Elizabeth introduced her new family, one by one. At each picture her friends prayed for each relative with thanksgiving, mentioning specifically what made each one so dear to Mary Elizabeth: a grandmother's wrinkly smile and warm, gentle presence; an impish uncle's way of telling stories; a niece's playfulness; a grandfather's strong and beautiful faith. The last picture showed Mary

Elizabeth herself in front of the Japanese house. She introduced herself for the first time in New York as Mariko and invited her friends to use her nickname from time to time. She didn't want to stop being Mary Elizabeth, but she did want to recognize how much she had come to treasure her heritage.

When they resumed their seats, Mary Elizabeth said that one of the best things was that the whole family in America and Japan were committed Christians, and their shared faith made the reunion even richer. One of her uncles is a pastor, and the family had shared Eucharist together in Japan. Afterward, her relatives had given Mary Elizabeth the pottery cup and plate used in the service. Even as Mary Elizabeth spoke, her pastor was filling the same pottery chalice with wine and putting a loaf of bread on the plate. These she set on a small table in the center of their circle.

The pastor reminded the ad hoc church that when they gathered around the table of the Lord, they were connected to Christians around the world.

They began their Eucharist with a familiar hymn from the Taizé community in France, a setting of Ephesians 4:4-6: "There is one Lord, one faith, one baptism . . . There is one God who is Father of all." The pastor reminded the ad hoc church that when they gathered around the table of the Lord, they were connected to Christians around the world. On this night she invited them to be particularly aware that, in Christ, they were connected with Mary Elizabeth's Japanese family, whose nearly life-sized faces surrounded them.

After sharing the bread and cup, the ad hoc church laid hands on Mary Elizabeth and prayed that she would continue to grow into her Japanese-American identity and that her integration would deepen. Once again they thanked God for her recent transformation. After a final hymn, the service ended by passing the peace—the Japanese way. Instead of the American custom of hugging, they bowed deeply and smiled to one another as they said, "May the peace of Christ be with you."

A delicious Japanese feast, catered by a neighborhood restaurant, was waiting for them when they finished. Everyone lingered over the food with good conversation and much laughter. Each person had been moved by what had happened to Mary Elizabeth and by the beautiful way she had chosen to share her experience. They began sharing what they knew of their own roots, and how the liturgy had reminded them of their own desire to claim their heritages more fully.

As for Mary Elizabeth, the New York Eucharist was the capstone of her Japan pilgrimage. "My celebration was just wonderful," she said, "and I'm so grateful for my friends' willingness to be there. That evening brought together various strands of my life and helped me see that God really wanted me to be healed. Everything we did seemed like a gift from God."

Recovery from Cancer

Eva was diagnosed with breast cancer at age forty. Her cancer was fast-growing and already fairly large when one day in the shower she first felt the lump. Immediately she was plunged into every woman's (and some men's) nightmare: The biopsy and waiting for results. Choosing a surgeon, and the surgery itself. The radiation and chemotherapy that sapped her strength and left her bald. Taking a medical leave from work. Hearing that her prognosis was not good.

Eva had always taken good care of her health. She ate nutritious meals, exercised, took her vitamins, and never missed a checkup. Understandably, she was angry with God, terrified for herself, and sad for her husband when cancer exploded life as she knew it. She could not bear to think about her children without a mother, nor could she imagine not living to see them grow up.

During this awful time Eva went to weekly healing services at her church and received the laying on of hands. For a few months nothing much seemed to change until one day when Eva was praying and weeping by herself. Suddenly into her turmoil came what she described as an "inaudible voice." It was as if God spoke directly into her soul without sound or even words. Eva understood and put her own words to the change she felt: "Start living right now."

Eva was weak and nauseous, but she took those words to heart. She began asking herself, "What do I really want to do today? What will I regret if I don't?" She began taking long walks and spending more time with her kids. She and her husband went away for a few honeymoon days. She volunteered to teach literacy skills at the local homeless shelter. She spoke frequently with good friends around the country. She invited some of them to visit, and they came, some flying in for just a day or two. She continued to attend the weekly healing services, and one evening the healing team came to her house. They gently put their hands on her as she lay on the couch, and prayed with her for several hours.

Slowly Eva's strength returned, and with it came a new hope for the future. She was already feeling better when a checkup confirmed that the remainder of her tumor was shrinking. A few months later, the tumor was undetectable, and against the odds, Eva was officially pronounced "in remission."

Six years later, Eva felt better than she had ever felt in her life. Her cancer had not returned. She had quit her previous job, one she hated. She now found great fulfillment being employed by the homeless shelter to direct the literacy program. She continued to spend much good time with her family. An enthusiastic member of the healing team at church, she was able to offer compassionate, nuanced, and well-grounded ministry to others with dire illnesses. Her motto was still, "Start living right now."

On the seventh anniversary of her diagnosis, Eva, her family, and the healing team (now dear friends) gathered for a free-form celebration of her recovery. Her church was temporarily without a pastor, but these dedicated laypeople didn't let that stop them. Eva asked her family and each member of the healing team to plan a special way to give thanks and praise, and to take turns leading the prayers.

That afternoon, in no particular order, they released "alleluia balloons" with prayers of thanksgiving. They laid hands on Eva and thanked God for her healing and for her new sense of ministry. They danced a wild and improvised dance with crepe paper streamers to Eva's favorite music, the first movement of an exuberant Mozart symphony, turned up very loud. One man read the story of Pentecost from Acts 2:1-21, how the Holy Spirit came like a rushing wind and transformed everyone present. He said Eva's story of the inaudible voice always reminded him of this story. His suggestion for prayer was that they make whooshing, windlike sounds, interspersed with "alleluia" and "thank you, Lord."

Eva's children wrote and read aloud special love letters to Eva, expressing how much she meant to them and including their own written heartfelt prayers of thanksgiving. Her husband gave Eva a beautiful bracelet with "Start living right now" etched on the inside. As he put it on her wrist, he prayed his own thanks, his face covered with tears. Eva wept with joy most of the afternoon.

Supper was a barbeque, well spiced with good talk, laughter, and music. Toward the end of the evening Eva said, "I could never have dreamed what it meant to be healed when I was first diagnosed. I was focused on just getting rid of the cancer, but that was only a part of my healing. I have been given my life back, yes, but my old life has been transformed into a new one. A really new one, and I'm so glad to be living it! Every day I thank God and ask God to show me the ministry I am to do today. And God shows me."

Rites of Passage

Jessica's Vows

Jessica was an unusually mature teenager who asked for a personal liturgy to celebrate earning her driver's license. She was excited about her new freedom but also aware of both her inexperience and the peer pressure she would face as a new driver. Jessica was not about to forget that acquaintances from school had been badly hurt in an accident the year before, an accident caused by carelessness and hijinks of friends in the backseat not wearing seat belts. (In her state the law allowed new drivers, even teenagers, to transport as many people as the car had seat belts.)

Jessica was familiar with the idea of personal healing liturgies, and her pastor was glad to help her plan "A Liturgy of Celebration and Responsibility." In about an hour their preparations were complete. Jessica invited two good friends to join her for the liturgy the following Saturday just before Jessica's first solo trip behind the wheel.

Although Jessica had a good relationship with her parents, she did not invite them. Wisely respecting Jessica's need to shape her liturgy in her own way, her parents did not fuss about being excluded. That Saturday they parked their car in the church parking lot and retreated.

The brief liturgy took place next to the car. The new license and the car keys sat on the dashboard in full view. Jessica's friends stood on each side as she responded to prepared questions she and the pastor had written together. Her vows took the following form:

Pastor: This is an important moment for you, Jessica, and a sign that you are becoming an adult. Do you promise to drive carefully and responsibly?

Jessica: I do.

Pastor: Do you promise that you will never mix driving and drinking?

Jessica: I do.

Pastor: Will you promise to always make sure all passengers have their seat belts fastened?

Jessica: I will.

Pastor: And will you try to find ways to use your driver's license to help others?

Jessica: I will, with the help of God.

Pastor (turning to Jessica's two friends): Will you two good friends promise to support Jessica in the vows she has just made, particularly when peer pressure is great?

Friends: We are glad to do so. And we celebrate this wonderful moment with Jessica.

The pastor then opened the door of the car, took the license and the keys, blessed them, and handed them to her. Jessica took the license and keys and held them in her open hands as the three prayed for her. The liturgy ended as she slid her new license into her wallet. At that moment she and her friends began jumping around the parking lot, whooping, "Yes! Yes! Yes! All riiight!"

Then they piled into the car, buckled up, and Jessica carefully drove away, her very first moment behind the wheel without an adult in the car. The three young women went to a restaurant and celebrated with much hilarity—and Jessica's two friends decided to ask for similar liturgies when they received their licenses.

Becoming a Man

In the weekly prison class on Gestalt Pastoral Care, the topic was healing.[1] The previous week we had discussed the concepts of individualized healing liturgies and had experienced the "Liturgy of Lies and Truth." This week I invited the eleven men to create a liturgy for someone in the class.

Curtis, a deeply committed Christian, quickly volunteered to be the focus of a healing liturgy. He told us that he had been feeling for a long time that he needed to give up his childish dependence on others to structure his life and make decisions for him. He explained, "I never rented my own apartment even though I had the money. Instead I stayed with people who had apartments. I never got my own driver's license. I just bummed rides from my friends. I never bought food for myself; I just ate out of other people's refrigerators. Someone else always got my jobs for me. Whatever I did, it was always, like, under someone else. I always needed someone to tell me what to do and when to do it. Some of the guys I followed were no good, and I did a lot of irresponsible and criminal stuff that hurt people. That's what landed me here in prison. And I've been carrying a lot of pain and guilt around, not talking about it and not letting it go. I want to grow up and be a real man, a man who knows himself and makes his own decisions."

As the class listened to Curtis, they realized that he was asking for a special rite of passage to usher him from his prolonged childhood into responsible manhood. He was also asking for a liturgy to proclaim cleansing from his guilt and offer hope of freedom from old expectations and habits. Finally, he wanted healing prayer regarding his chaotic and emotionally damaging childhood.

A large order. Before we began working with Curtis to shape a personalized liturgy for him, I stressed again that a healing liturgy is not magic, but it could express Curtis's desire for healing, our support for him, and God's desire to heal. We could trust that God would hear our prayers and would work in us to open Curtis to the particular healing God had in mind for him. It was not our liturgy that would change Curtis, but Curtis's continued cooperation with God's power.

None of the men had ever planned a liturgy, and some were skeptical at first that a liturgy could offer anything of value. Furthermore, our classroom is not really conducive to liturgy. It is a small, strictly institutional space in need of paint, with worn chairs, locked bookcases, chalkboards, bare windows, a few struggling plants, and the ugliest metal teacher's desk I've ever seen. There is always noise outside our door, sometimes making it difficult to hear one another. Not much to work with to create a meaningful physical setting, and precious little to use as symbols of transformation.

Even so, our room is a sanctuary of sorts. Correctional officers almost never enter, and our room has become a place of laughter, challenge, learning, hard work, hope, discovery, pride, and increasing trust among the members of the class. With that going for us, the liturgy that emerged from this group—not all of whom are Christians—was one of astonishing beauty, creativity, and psychological and spiritual depth.

I contributed some ideas at first, but soon it became clear that the class was entering wholeheartedly into the planning with Curtis. Something seemed to ignite in them, and suddenly they were thinking about liturgical flow with sensitivity and theological sophistication. In the end they themselves put it together and told me what my part was. After careful listening to Curtis and much discussion, their plan for Curtis's liturgy was written on the board:

<u>A Rite of Passage</u>
Opening Prayer
Surrender
Cleansing
Turning Around
Claiming
Presentation
Closing Prayer

The service began with Curtis sitting in a chair in the front of the room. Directly in front of him was a wastebasket. Facing him, about twelve feet away, was an empty chair. Beside Curtis stood Joe, a man chosen by Curtis to symbolize and embody Christ. For most of the liturgy, "Christ" had his hand on Curtis's shoulder. As "The Rev," I was told to stand on the other side of Curtis. On the desk behind us was placed a large, healthy philodendron, the one thing in the room that might conceivably be seen as a symbol of renewal. This beautiful plant, which hadn't been in our room before that night, was to represent the gift of manhood and new life.

Just before we began the liturgy, Curtis announced that from now on he wanted to be addressed by his given name, not the nickname given to him in prison. "I want to be who I really am," he said, "and I want people to treat me like the man I'm going to be." His statement caught the essence of the movement of grace in him, and our part in it. I thought it was a wonderful call to worship.

I opened with a prayer that God would guide our liturgy and allow healing mercy to flow to Curtis. I asked that God speak through our actions and shape our words, and that Curtis be open to grace and newness. With halting voice Curtis elaborated on his desire to surrender all that had held him hostage; his sharing was both a confession of sin and an expression of pain and need. We were moved by his courageous honesty and vulnerability as he spoke of his life, surrendering it as best he could to God's mercy and healing. In summary he tossed into the wastebasket a bit of dirt, symbolizing his sin and bad choices, and then pieces of paper on which he had written the words *Guilt, Irresponsibility, Lies,* and *Childishness.* As he wadded up each paper, he said, "I reject guilt!" . . . "I reject irresponsibility!" . . . "I especially reject lies!" . . . "I reject childishness!" With each toss, the ad hoc congregation responded with "Amen!"

When I anointed Curtis as a sign of cleansing and forgiveness, he began to weep. I briefly spoke of how God could heal his pain and make things new. God could erase the chalkboard and give new chances. I referred to the story of the returning prodigal son, whose father rushed joyously toward him and offered him new clothes, a ring, and a celebration. Then I formally assured Curtis of forgiveness in the name of the Father, Son, and Holy Spirit. As I finished, Curtis sat for several moments in silence, breathing deeply, his eyes closed. Then he looked up at us with shining eyes and exclaimed, "I feel like a ton of bricks just came off my shoulders!"

Next, six men stood up and, along with "Christ," ushered Curtis across the room with great ceremony to the empty chair. "Christ" looked into his eyes and said solemnly, "Curtis, it's time to turn around now and be a man." Slowly and thoughtfully Curtis turned himself around and sat in his new place. "Christ" poured water on Curtis's hands as another sign of cleansing from his past, and said, "Curtis, you don't have to be bound by your past any longer. It is cleansed from you now. I want you to be a real man, my real man."

Brian, chosen to be the "presenter," approached the philodendron, picked it up, and spontaneously began chanting "ohmmm, ohmmm, ohmmm," as he said, "to mark the sacredness of our ritual." Holding the plant high above his head, he brought it to Curtis with great ceremony. As he placed it in Curtis's arms, he said: "Curtis, receive this sign of your new life as a real man. Let your new manhood be like a tree of life. Just as this plant grew from a seed and blossomed, let your new manhood grow and blossom."

He handed the plant to Curtis, who hugged it to himself, nearly engulfed in the lush greenness and shimmering silence. Those of us in the ad hoc church recognized that something momentous was happening to Curtis, and we were content to wait for several minutes.

Just as I was beginning to wonder how to move things along, "Christ" said gently to Curtis: "I'm going to hold this plant for you now because you are going to need your hands free to do things for me. But I'll always be here, and whenever you need to be reminded that you are a man, I'll give it back for you to hold for a few minutes. You are going to make mistakes, but I'll help you learn how to be a responsible, faithful, and loving man, and you can trust that I am always here right with you."

I led a closing prayer as all of us laid our hands on Curtis. We prayed that Curtis would be empowered to live his manhood and learn more deeply what it means to be a Christian man. We prayed that God would strengthen what had happened in the liturgy. We prayed for his continued healing, especially regarding his painful childhood, and again asked that we be used to support Curtis as he learned his new identity. Finally we gave thanks for what had happened to Curtis that night, and for the faithful presence of the Holy One with us.

After the service, the men were eager to give feedback to Curtis. Their responses took the form of sharing their own experience of growing up in prison. Some warned that the old clichés that proclaim that real men aren't soft, weak, emotional, and certainly not tearful, are simply dead wrong. They were adamant that men need to cry, to hurt, to need, to feel, and they urged Curtis to cherish these parts of himself.

Nearly all of them stressed the importance of responsibility and fidelity and challenged Curtis to grow up. Rod summed it up well: "This service was not playing around, Curtis. This was serious and important and for the rest of your life. Now the hard work begins for you. You can't get away with letting your responsibilities go any longer. It's going to be real easy to slip back into your old ways, but that's where commitment comes in. You have to keep at it even when you don't feel like it."

Most gave similar advice, much of it demanding and rigid. Some of their feedback seemed downright harsh to me, as if they were saying that no mistakes are allowed. Usually I remind people sharing their response to a liturgy to simply tell what they themselves experienced, without preaching or judging. But I didn't interrupt this time because I had a strong feeling that these men lived in a world of which I had no firsthand experience and were working out Curtis's rite of passage in their own way. I did give my own feedback, expressing how greatly moved I was by this liturgy. I also told Curtis that he was certain to slip and make mistakes, but a real man learns from his mistakes. He will not be perfect, and he will be learning to be a man until he dies.

As the feedback continued, most offered to be there for Curtis. Rod said, "You had the liturgy; it was made for you. But because we were all witnesses to it, now all of us are involved. As witnesses and participants, we have a responsibility too—to help you stick to your resolve. We have to be true to our responsibility as witnesses."

Curtis listened with great attention to everything his friends said. Then he replied, "At first I felt judged by what you were saying, but then I saw that you were telling me what my new life is going to be like. You're giving me the benefit of your experience. I like that you didn't just make me feel good; you said some things I needed to hear. This was the real deal. Thank you for that."

He then broke into an enormous smile and said, "I feel so thankful that I have some brothers who will stand by me but won't do it [my work] for me. I'm grateful to God, too, for this healing. I feel wonderful and, like, new."

As Curtis finished speaking, no one said anything for a few moments. A bit astonished by what had just happened among us, some murmured about how they were moved and awed; others said they were frankly stunned by the power of God working through us. Simultaneously energized, excited, and oddly tired, we ebbed into comfortable and reflective silence.

A week later we were ready to talk some more. Carlos said, "I was so moved [to know] that even in this dull, depressing place, God can work. And we can find a way to make something beautiful." José said, "I was just planning to go through it, you know, like a class, but then, after the opening prayer, it all became so real." Brian reflected, "It made me consider some issues I'd like to deal with. I think I need something like this myself, but I don't know yet if I have the courage."

Curtis was still glowing from the effects of his liturgy. He was feeling his way into his new identity, loving his new sense of himself. He said he had seen Rod's face all week in his imagination, and heard his straight talk about responsibility every time he was tempted to slide into old patterns of behavior and thought. He told us that one night he had gone to the gym to work out, and another man tried to pick a fight with him: "Yo, Curtis, you got a problem with me?" Instead of escalating the tension with verbal retaliation, Curtis spoke to him from a new position of quiet strength: "No, my brother. I have no problem with you. Actually, I was just watching you work out." The other man was disarmed, the two begin talking, and the man wound up telling Curtis that he had been under a lot of pressure lately and that "you don't have to worry about anything from me."

Curtis finished telling this story. Then he looked around the room, smiling. "I couldn't have done it without you," he said.

A Service of Endings and Beginnings

My husband, George McClain, and I adapted "A Service of Endings and Beginnings" to celebrate his parents' retirement in 1976.[2] When Ralph took early retirement from his job as principal and beloved "grandpa" of an elementary school, Dora decided to resign from her job as a school librarian in Fort Wayne. Their immediate plan was to volunteer for a year at McCurdy School, a United Methodist institution in New Mexico primarily serving Hispanic children. Having worked hard all their lives, now they wanted to share their experience and expertise and do some of the things they had always dreamed about.

Since we knew Dora and Ralph well, and since we created this service as a Christmas gift, we didn't consult them ahead of time, although we left the details open to their scrutiny and change. Sensing that the very fact of having a special retirement service would be a new, and maybe disconcerting, idea for them, we kept it simple and familiar; the liturgy consisted of Bible readings interspersed with short liturgical affirmations, a bit of spontaneous sharing, and a prayer of sending forth. We also told them that as far as we were concerned, the service didn't have to take place at all, but we would give the printed copy to them anyway as a statement of our support and love for them during this momentous change, and as a sign of our continued prayers for their new adventure.

They decided to go ahead. As Dora said, "We were agreeably surprised and delighted."

The service, which George led, took place in their living room in the late spring, just before their jobs ended for good. In preparation George's sister, craftswoman Jane Gear, made a marvelous banner, which showed a pathway to McCurdy School flanked by two trees. On one tree was a list of all the schools Ralph had served as teacher and principal. On the other was Ralph's often-repeated motto, which perfectly summed up his philosophy. It said, "The reward for good work is more good work to do."

George and I made another banner—not nearly as artistic as Jane's—based on the story in Genesis in which the aged Sarah is told she would bear a child. Upon hearing God's crazy-sounding promise, Sarah collapsed in laughter because she and Abraham "were old, advanced in age; it had ceased to be with Sarah after the manner of women" (Gen. 18:11). Our banner showed the silhouette of an elderly and very pregnant woman with a phrase taken from Genesis, "Sarah laughed."

With the banners hung, and a huge armload of lilacs beautifully perfuming the family room, all was ready. Across the street, in the church, tables were set for a catered dinner afterward, decorated with pots of marigolds Dora would later plant in their garden.

Their service began with a "Statement of the Occasion":

George: We are assembled here today to commemorate a turning point in the journey of Ralph and Dora. In our biblical tradition endings and beginnings have special significance.

Ad Hoc Church: We recall how Abraham and Sarah set out for a new country and a new life, not knowing where they were being led.

George: We recall how Jesus left his carpenter's tools, ventured out into the desert, and there laid hold of his new vocation.

Ad Hoc Church: We recall how the fishermen left their nets, and how women left their traditional roles, to follow Jesus in his itinerant ministry.

George: We are gathered here to offer thanksgiving for the life that Ralph and Dora have led over the years—in school teaching and administration, in library work, in the raising of a family, and in community and church life. Many chapters are now coming to a close. However, a most important chapter, a new venturing forth, is about to begin. We gather to celebrate their past, to support their new undertaking, and to ask God to bless their journey into the desert.

After singing the hymn "God of Our Life," the group entered into a time of sharing called "The Past Remembered." The printed program invited those gathered to "share recollections of significant points or characteristics of the journey Dora and Ralph have made thus far—with family and friends, at various schools and libraries, at church, and in the community." And so this little group of old friends and close family did what they usually did when together: they told stories. Some were moving, some funny, others inspiring, piecing together memories of Dora and Ralph's many gifts and contributions over the years.

Then came two scripture readings. George introduced the first (Gen. 12:1-8) by saying, "In the following passage Abraham and Sarah are called to move to a new country because God is going to 'make of you a great nation . . . and in you all the families of the earth shall be blessed.'" When Abraham heard this call, he was seventy-five years old! Before the second reading George said, "Sarah also experienced how there is no age beyond which God cannot give birth to new capacities within us," and someone read from Genesis 17:15-19 and 18:10-15 the prediction of Sarah's old-age pregnancy.

Again George invited sharing; everyone was asked to express to Ralph and Dora any hopes, wishes, and prayers for their new undertaking. There was much support for them all around, and admiration for their courage to leave all that was familiar and dear, including their comfortable house, to live in a small trailer in the hot, cold, and dusty desert for a year. Congratulatory letters and telegrams sent for the occasion were also read and put away to treasure later.

Finally came the part that Dora said she loved best of all. Dora and Ralph were liturgically sent forth to embrace their new life. The two of them were invited to stand in the middle of the room, and everyone put hands on them as the ad hoc church prayed together:

> "O God who has brought us through valleys, over mountains, and across deserts to this place, we ask you to guide us along our way in the days and months ahead. Especially we ask that you be present to Dora and Ralph in their new life and new mission. Grant them the assurance of faith as they venture out into a new country as a modern-day Abraham and Sarah. May they discern new forms of usefulness at McCurdy School this next year and wherever they are led in successive years. In work and play, in sickness and health, in dark times and joyful times, guide them in their path, O God. In the name of Jesus Christ, who taught us to pray . . ." (At this point we said the Lord's Prayer.)
>
> "The Lord bless you and keep you, the Lord make his face to shine upon you and be gracious to you; the Lord lift up the light of his countenance on you and give you peace. Amen."

In the years after retiring, Dora and Ralph returned to McCurdy School for two more stints of volunteering. They also traveled; tutored; helped folks with their taxes; attended Elderhostel events; nurtured rich friendships; made gorgeous liturgical banners; served in various capacities at church; offered gracious hospitality; loved and supported their children, grandchildren, and great-grandchildren. Ralph died in 1993, and six years later Dora moved to an assisted living apartment, where she remains keen, witty, active, and wise.

In 2005 I asked Dora, then ninety-three, to comment on that long-ago retirement service some thirty years earlier. She said, "It was really nice. There was a good group here with a bunch of friends and family and Ralph's school colleagues, including the superintendent of schools. People were given parts to read, and everyone had something to say during the sharing parts. I liked the Abraham and

Sarah theme. You know, we always referred to my parents as Abraham and Sarah because they left their Mennonite community in Switzerland and settled here in Indiana. Neither of them ever went back to Europe again.

"I really liked the service. We even referred to it ten years later in the invitations to our golden wedding celebration. "

We chatted some more, and then Dora added, "Tell your readers I liked the service *a lot*. I've always been one for a bit of ceremony!"

Liturgies of Vocational Blessing

⚛

A Ministry of Car Repair

After much prayerful discernment, Jeff was convinced that his gift for fixing things was a vocation from God. He had been a car mechanic since he was a young man, and now he was about to open his own garage. Jeff wanted it to be not only a place where cars would find new life, but also a place where Jesus the Carpenter would be honored. Jeff did not necessarily mean that he would use his garage to preach to customers or slip them printed material about his church. He might do those things, but that was not his primary concern. Instead he wanted to promise to be the very best mechanic he could be, always keeping in mind that auto repair is a crucial service to the community, a job that can be offered in the name of Christ.

Jeff was passionate about the stewardship of repairing old cars that still had miles left in them. He planned to use about a tenth of his time resurrecting these "throwaways," cars one step from the junkyard. He would fix and then sell dinged-up but usable cars very cheaply to low-income people who needed transportation to work. He also planned to maintain these cars for a small fraction of the usual cost. He would charge nothing for labor, and he would buy most of the used parts himself.

In Jeff's special liturgy, held in his new garage, the ad hoc congregation formally celebrated that God had gifted Jeff with mechanical ability, and they acknowledged that repairing cars was his Christian vocation. At one point in the liturgy, each person held one of his wrenches, blessed it in turn, and then placed it next to bread and wine on an "altar"—a desk that had been cleared for the occasion. The ad hoc congregation prayed that the garage would be a place where God dwells. They laid their hands on Jeff's head and prayed that God would bless him and his work. After they shared Eucharist, the service ended with the sprinkling of water and a blessing in each area of the new building.

Jeff's service of dedication to a "ministry of auto mechanics" was profoundly important to his Christian growth, for the memory of his liturgy continued to remind him daily of his call to a unique ministry. Those present as his ad hoc church were not only inspired by Jeff's Christian commitment but also quite excited by his "cars for the poor" project. "Jeff's idea of tithing his time and skill is something I've never thought of," one said. "I'd like to help some way. I'll contribute to his spare-parts kitty." Others agreed, and although Jeff's liturgy was in no way a fund-raising event, before the day was over, Jeff's ad hoc church had established both a fund and a committee to help him buy the spare parts he would need.

The Dedication of a Musical Career

Barbara, a classical musician, felt that her spiritual journey was leading her both to be baptized and, at the same time, to formally dedicate her musical career to God. This idea was no momentary whim for Barbara; together we had discerned this call over a period of many months and had carefully planned her liturgy. So it was that a small group of friends gathered at her house one evening to witness her vows and support her in taking these important steps in her spiritual life.

We met in her music room, where Barbara had placed a bowl of water on a table near her beautiful grand piano. Her baptism, which followed the order in *The United Methodist Book of Worship*, was a high point for Barbara; she had wanted to do this for a long time.

The ad hoc church was moved by the simplicity of the baptismal service, and especially by Barbara's glowing smile.

Hair and face still wet, Barbara spoke of her lifelong love of music and of many childhood hours happily spent at the keyboard. She publicly thanked God for her musical ability, and for the gift of music itself. Then she made the following vow she had written:

> "On this day I dedicate my music to God. I promise to allow my music to give pleasure, and to play in a way that invites my audiences into the deepest parts of themselves. I promise to play not so much for career advancement but for God's glory. I will play both 'sacred' and 'secular' music, because I understand that great depth of beauty can, in itself, direct us toward God, even when God is not precisely named. I ask God to help me, and you to pray for me."

After her promises we laid hands on her, asking for God's blessing and guidance in her vocation as musician. We asked that she be enabled to find her way as a Christian musician with musical colleagues who might not understand her spirituality. We thanked God for the grace that brought her to this point of dedication.

Next we shared the bread and wine of Eucharist and a hymn, after which Barbara played a beautiful Beethoven sonata for us, a gift that indeed "invited us into the deepest parts of ourselves." We ended her celebration with a delicious dinner she had prepared.

Six years after the liturgy, Barbara reported that the effects of the liturgy were still with her. "Having that liturgy really makes a difference in the way I make music," she told me. "I think of it all the time, and it reminds me that my music belongs to God. That was a wonderful evening."[3]

Liturgies of Commissioning

⊷

First Steps toward a New Project

At an Opening to Grace workshop, Judith told the group that she needed to work on her marriage. About to turn fifty, Judith suddenly realized that her life had been almost entirely organized around meeting the needs of her husband and children. Until recently she had found great fulfillment in cooking, cleaning, and other household tasks, but now housework felt like drudgery. She made it clear that while her husband was not a tyrant demanding that Judith serve him, she still felt bound by habit and tradition to continue doing all the household work. This was true, even though the children were long gone and her husband was semiretired and in good health.

Although she loved her sweet husband dearly, she strongly felt the stirrings of change, of wanting to recast her life in a new pattern. She had long held a secret dream of opening a fabric store in her small town and organizing classes there on a variety of subjects, from needlecrafts to parenting. She envisioned it as a place where the coffeepot would always be on, a place of refuge and welcome, where women could meet to talk and work on projects together, a place where preschoolers would have a play area of their own. Judith had her own small nest egg from a recent inheritance and could spend it on getting her project started. As she explored and prayed with the workshop group, it seemed to her that Jesus was smiling and pointing to her store, inviting her to go ahead. Judith knew she would take this prayer image seriously and would continue to discern about her new venture in the months ahead until she was certain that she was really being called to her fabric store project.

Despite not yet knowing the details, Judith was sure that God was inviting her to a new stage in her life, a time of expansion and discovery, a time of birthing something new. Everything seemed to be falling into place: her dream, an apparent call from God, the start-up money. But the first step down this new path was to talk to her husband about her dream and ask him to share the household tasks. Although she was pretty sure her husband would assume half of the household work with little complaint, Judith felt oddly reluctant and a little scared. She said, "I guess the reason I came to this retreat was to see if I could find the courage to change things with my husband. I know I have to talk to him, and I'm pretty sure he will be supportive after he gets over being surprised out of his mind. I've been trying for months to get up the courage to broach the subject. I don't get why talking to the man I love is such a big deal."

After a little Gestalt work, Judith quickly realized that embracing her dream meant giving up a familiar role, one she was really good at. It had given her life meaning for years and earned her admiration from other women in her small town. Sharing household tasks would mean that she would have to surrender her high standards of a spotless house, of meals always cooked to perfection, and of ironing done up just so. Continuing to define herself solely as a homemaker felt safe and was a perfect way to ensure that she would not have to risk doing something new.

Judith saw how easy it would be to just drift along, letting things stay the way they were in her marriage, so again she asked the retreat group to pray for her to have the courage to do what she knew she must. I proposed that we create a short liturgy of surrendering her old role as homemaker and commissioning her to speak to her husband. Judith enthusiastically agreed.

The ad hoc church and I quickly helped Judith plan her special service, and together we rounded up the symbolic objects Judith had chosen. These included a vacuum cleaner, an iron, a coffeepot, a pair of scissors, a few yards of fabric, her wedding ring, a towel and a basin of water, and anointing oil. These items were placed on or near a small table in the middle of the room.

The liturgy began with a hymn and a prayer for guidance. Then Judith touched the vacuum and the iron and spoke to them. "Vacuum and iron, you are symbols of housekeeping, symbols of how I defined my life up to now. I appreciate how useful you are, and I am not rejecting you. I will still use you, but just not as much. You are no longer my vocation! I am moving on!" Then Judith put the two appliances in a closet and shut the door.

Smiling hugely, she sat down in the circle again. Then, fingering the coffeepot, scissors, and fabric, she said to the group, "These symbolize my dream of a special fabric store. I've wanted to acknowledge my dream for a long time. I think my dream may even be a call! I'm placing my dream on the altar now, and I ask that God will either shape my dream into a call or let my dream die. I am ready to do something else if that is what God wants." Then she prayed, "God, show me the way. Please." The group responded, "Amen!"

One of the ad hoc church, a clergyperson, picked up the wedding ring and led Judith in taking the following vow:

Minister: Judith, you first put this ring on your finger thirty-two years ago. On that day you promised in front of witnesses and in the presence of God to love, honor, and cherish Jack. Do those vows still hold for you?

Judith: Oh yes!

Minister: Are you willing to love, honor, and cherish Jack enough to share with him your dream? Will you ask him to share the housework?

Judith (in tears): Yes, I am. I am ready to talk to him now, and I ask God to help me.

As Judith put her ring back on her finger, the ad hoc church gathered around and put their hands on her.

Minister: Judith, you have asked us to pray that you will have courage to speak to your husband about your dream of a special fabric store. In the name of Christ we pray together that you will be empowered to share your heart with Jack.

He paused, and several other members of the church prayed aloud for Judith.

Minister (anointing Judith): Judith, we in this small congregation commission you in the name of the Father, the Son, and the Holy Spirit to do what you yourself know you must. Go and speak to Jack with our support and love.

Judith: I am grateful for this commission from this little church. I am going to tell Jack that for many years I was happy (most of the time) to raise the kids and wash clothes, dishes, woodwork, and floors. Now the Lord is calling me to something new, some new way to serve, a new way to use my skills. I am going to have some kind of ministry outside the house, maybe in a fabric store. Whatever shape my ministry takes, for the next stage of my life I'm going to wash feet!

Judith picked up the towel and basin. Slowly, lovingly, and attentively, she washed the feet of her new friends who had become church for her. As she continued this remarkable action around the room, her breathing deepened, her face looked more relaxed, and her energy focused and settled. When she was finished, she looked up and said, "I haven't felt this clear or this excited in years. I know the Lord will make it plain what I am to do next after I speak to Jack. Thank you so much!"

Becoming a Mennonite Wild Woman

Bonnie was diagnosed with uterine fibroids so extensive that the only medical option was to have her uterus removed. Her fibroids were like tangled ropes snaking through her uterus, wrapping tightly around its outside, and firmly binding her uterus to her abdominal wall.

For Bonnie, losing her uterus without a fight was unthinkable. As she put it, "They don't castrate men, so why should I be castrated?" Resolving to work holistically with her "bound uterus," she promptly took six weeks off to be alone, reasoning that if she had the recommended hysterectomy, people would surely leave her alone for that much time. Using therapy, journaling, and prayer, she focused intensely on personal growth issues of emotions and spirit. After her brief "sabbatical," she maintained her fierce commitment to inner work. Six months into her fight for her uterus, Bonnie had clearly made a great deal of progress, both emotionally and spiritually. Best of all, she had had two regular menstrual cycles of twenty-eight days, something that had not occurred in years.

Bonnie was elated by this progress, but she knew more work was needed and that "something is keeping me from taking the next step in my growth." She came to an Opening to Grace retreat to see if she could discover her next step.

I asked her if she would be willing to pretend to be one inch tall and imaginatively explore what was going on with her uterus. She agreed to this bit of Gestalt work, and almost immediately began to see vivid images of a tangled mass of "strings" tightly bound around her uterus, which now seemed about six feet high. Bonnie, a take-charge woman, immediately tried imaginatively to cut the strings apart. But she couldn't do it. The strings were too strong for her. When she invited God to join her there in front of her uterus, she felt herself being shown that the strings could quite easily be *untied*. She also felt God's invitation to untie the strings herself; somehow she knew that this was her work to do.

The clear images were exciting and hopeful to Bonnie, but to her great surprise, she felt oddly reluctant about moving ahead. She who had worked so hard to get well in body, mind, and spirit now was experiencing timidity, trepidation, and actual fear. I asked her what might happen if she went ahead. As she mused about what might happen if she actually untied the ropes that bound her uterus, she found herself talking about much more than her physical body.

"Well, if I untie the strings I'd have a lot of string to clean up. It would be a big mess, but I'd be free. I'd be unbound.

"But if I were unbound, everything would change! I would have to change! And people I care about would be really upset and mad at me if I moved out of my old roles. They might really be scandalized and freaked out if I said what I really think! They might not be able to handle it. And I really love the people in my church. I don't want to hurt them or be in their faces in a mean way."

Bonnie paused, her face both thoughtful and animated.

"If I untied those strings, I'd have to make up a whole new dance for my life! I'd become a wild woman!"

With these words came a huge discovery. Bonnie saw that her bound uterus was a perfect symbolic picture of how she felt as a Mennonite, bound by historically rigid roles for women. As Bonnie put it, it was as if her very womanhood was in chains, chains she had been in all her life, iron chains that were hard to identify because they were so gently applied. She recalled being told that girls couldn't be pastors or astronauts or doctors, and that being a wife and mother was surely God's only loving will for her. She was carefully—and affectionately—schooled to be quiet and unassertive. She was nurtured by church and culture to be interested only in "women's concerns," and taught that Christian women should always be under the "headship" of men.

She was absolutely right that getting free could have some far-reaching consequences. I suggested that she sit with this dilemma for a few minutes and invite God to help her know what to do. Had she really heard God's direction in her images of the easily untied strings and in her subsequent discovery of their meaning? If so, was now the right time to untie them?

The workshop group prayed silently for Bonnie and gave her some space. Soon Bonnie looked up, her chin determined, face pink, and eyes snapping with passion. She spoke with a new firmness.

"I've known for a long time that God has been calling me to help women and girls claim their freedom in Christ. I know I'm supposed to speak the truth to them about who they are. I need to do this under God's direction, and with love, but I also know I will shake up the Mennonite Church. It may not be pleasant, but I'm going to stop worrying about what everyone thinks, and follow God's call. I'm going to do it! I won't be bound anymore! I'm untying the strings! God wants me to be a wild woman!"

At this point Bonnie had reached some clarity, a resting place in her growth journey where she could pause to assimilate and live into this new place. However, she would soon return home, where she might not have much support for this new path. Her good work at the retreat might be hard to hold on to without church support. I proposed that we create a brief liturgy to help undergird and strengthen her work. Our aim would be to give Christian recognition both to her call to be a Mennonite wild woman, and to the reality that her call was still being shaped. Our liturgy would perhaps be an icon for her to recall later as she lived into her new identity.

Bonnie loved this idea, so in a few minutes the ad hoc church had planned a liturgy with her to express her very own healing journey. We worked hard to get the wording to suit Bonnie's way of speaking, and to create the liturgy in keeping with her own inner world and her Mennonite tradition.

Bonnie's liturgy was short and simple. Another Mennonite woman in the group, asked to "stand in" for the Mennonite Church, silently anointed Bonnie's forehead with oil and kept her hands on Bonnie's head for the rest of the liturgy as a sign of Bonnie's being touched by God in a special way for personal growth and a special task. A pastor then slowly prayed the carefully constructed prayer created by Bonnie and the other participants:

Creator, Healer, Stringpuller, Mother,
Stir up in this woman, Bonnie, the power to speak against all the
 "can'ts" for women,
  to bring deliverance to the captives,
  and above all, to have the power to create a new dance.
Amen.

As Bonnie heard the prayer, she looked up, her eyes fiery, and told us that she was electrified by what she called "Solid Truth." "I know in an even deeper way that my wild woman call is true," she said. "I can actually see myself dancing a new dance." Then the rest of us prayed for her continued physical healing and that she would be encouraged to find out what it means to be a wild woman dancing her new dance. As we were praying for her, a workshop participant began singing a simple and rhythmic Native American chant:

Thank you for this day, Lord,
Thank you for this day.
Thank you for this day, Lord,
Thank you for this day.
This healing, this healing, this healing day!

Someone picked up a drum, and spontaneously the nine of us began to move to the music—a sign of our participation in Bonnie's "new dance." Some cut loose in ways that surprised them. Perhaps Bonnie's brief liturgy had released more than one wild woman!

I spoke to Bonnie five weeks after the workshop. She said that she had had two more normal-length periods that were not fraught with her usual severe PMS. She had lost seventeen pounds and felt wonderful. She was amazed at how often she was saying, "I can!" instead of her familiar "I can't." Again and again she was discovering that things that once seemed impossible were indeed possible. The wild-woman seeds were sprouting.

Liturgies of Declaration

Good Enough!

Carole entered ordained ministry after many years as a competent and well-loved schoolteacher. When she first began to have some glimmers of her call to ministry, her immediate reaction was old and familiar: "Who, me? I'm not enough for that." Whenever this doubt niggled at her, she usually sensed Jesus telling her, "I'll make you enough." After careful and long discernment, Carole became convinced at last that both her call and Jesus' encouragement were genuine. So, in faith she gathered her courage, quit her job, sold her house to pay for her theological education, and enrolled in seminary.

Carole was ordained upon graduation and began serving a series of small congregations, some of them already known to church officials as troubled and difficult. Most of the members of her churches responded well to Carole, but, as so often happens, in each church there was a small group that opposed her ministry. Some complained that she was "too smiley and touchy-feely"; others said she was "too biblically focused." Subsequently she was edged out of three churches by these groups. Nevertheless Carole poured her energy and passion into pastoring her flocks faithfully and lovingly. Daily she prayed for her people.

Carole was near the mandatory retirement age when her denominational board told her there would be no more pastorates for her.

They suggested that she might want to return to the classroom. Carole was devastated and hurt. Who would she be if she wasn't a pastor? She had given up everything to follow her call to ministry and had regarded the denomination's appointment system as God's will for her life. Suddenly all the rejections from a few church members plus the rejection of the denominational board magnified and merged with long-dormant rejections from her childhood. She found herself deflated, defeated, flattened. As her bubbly energy drained away, she recognized she was in danger of sinking into real depression. Although experienced in working with her inner growth, she could not work or journal or pray her way out of her funk. She returned to her therapist to deal with her hurt and anger, but not much changed for her. In fact, despite her hard work, her old inner tape of "I'm not enough" began playing again with astonishing volume.

Carole came to an Opening to Grace workshop in the hopes of finding a way through this tangle. As she shared her recent events with us, she said, "Even when I was feeling the most wretched, I never really doubted my call. I just lost the energy to fight for it. But I see that I've developed a mighty sore spot in regard to criticism that's sending me into a tailspin. I think I've been holding on to my old identity of 'not enough' as a way to avoid the risks of finding another way to be a minister."

It seemed to me that Carole had reached a point of clarity in her growth, but she had also hit a wall in regard to going forward. She was stuck.

Carole herself said, "I've done all I could. Now I have to depend on God to do the rest." She paused. "It's time to let go of that old 'not enough' tape. I've worked on that a lot, and now it's really time." As a Gestalt Pastoral Care trainee, Carole had often participated in personal liturgies for others, and very creatively too. Now she asked the group to help her create a liturgy of her own. She thought that the "Lies and Truth" form fit her perfectly. Her idea was to be anointed and then hear affirmations of the gospel as it impacted her "not enough" tape.

Carole's three lies were variations of the theme of "not enough." We listed them on newsprint:

1. I am not good enough, period.
2. I'm certainly not good enough for ministry.
3. My ministry is over.

After a little more planning together, we were ready to begin. First we offered a prayer of preparation and blessing of the oil.

"O Lord, help us to hear your words of truth for Carole. Show us what to say, and let our words find a home in her hurting heart. Let our words carry your healing balm, and let the truth push out old tapes that are not of you. We ask you to bless this oil as a sign of the Holy Spirit. As it soaks into Carole's skin, we ask that your truth soak in as well. We pray in the name of Jesus. Amen."

Then each of us anointed Carole in turn, using her own carefully chosen words:

"Carole, I anoint you in the name of God who created you, Christ who calls you, and the Holy Spirit who empowers you."

Each person present anointed Carole, then identified one damaging message as a lie, and, while holding her hands and looking into her eyes, spoke a sentence or two of gospel truth to her.

It's important to note that we did not see our function as evaluating her competence for ordained ministry or deciding whether or not the denominational board had made a mistake. That was not our job. Furthermore, we were not simply trying to make her feel better by taking her side. Nor were we trying to convince Carole that she had somehow done something wrong. We were simply proclaiming the gospel as best we could to Carole in a personal and non-judgmental way.

Naming Carole's lies and proclaiming the truth mostly consisted of repeating Carole's own words back to her. We were depending on God to work through this liturgical action to plant the truth more deeply in Carole's emotions and spirit.

"Carole, you have long been led to believe that you are not enough. In the name of Jesus Christ, I proclaim that to be a lie. Amen! The plain and simple truth is that in Christ you are enough! Amen!

"Carole, you have been treated by many as if you are not enough. I proclaim that that, too, is a lie. Carole, since you are a Christian, I believe that God dwells in you, and because of that, you are abundantly, overflowingly enough. Amen!

"Carole, when you were called to ministry, your reaction was, 'I'm not enough for that.' Carole, as a member of the body of Christ, I claim that to be a lie. The truth is that when God calls you to ministry, God also empowers you to do it. God tells you who you are. Jesus makes you enough. Amen!

"Carole, during your childhood you took in all the negative comments and negative attitudes that told you that you were no good. Be assured that this terrible lie is not from the loving God who created you. The truth is that you are a beautiful and beloved child of God, full of promise and potential. Amen!

"Carole, the suggestion that you return to teaching, along with the criticism from some folks in your churches, sent the message that your ministry is over. In the name of Jesus, that is a lie! The truth is that God will not desert you now. God will help you find your way as a minister. Amen!"

About halfway through our proclamations, Carole got thirsty and asked for a drink of water. With Carole's permission this casual request was incorporated into the liturgy. The water was brought to her in a Communion chalice, and she was invited to "drink in" each affirmation as she heard it, taking a fresh sip of water and some deep breaths as each person spoke. We paused between each lie/truth pair until Carole was ready to go on. As we finished, Carole asked that group members write down what they had said so she could assimilate and treasure what she received. This we did, sending her home with affirmations for her "memory box."

Her liturgy ended with the laying on of hands and prayer for

Carole's continued healing, and that God would open some new doors of ministry to her.

Two months later Carole was working as a part-time hospital chaplain. She joyfully told me of her new job, "I love it! It feels absolutely right." She went on to say, "After the liturgy, I had the courage to apply for the chaplaincy job. I'm not sure I could have done that before, given the state I was in. The liturgy was the turning point. Afterward, when I heard about my present job, I felt, 'Okay, I know I have the gifts for this ministry. If God wants it, it will happen.' I know that my worth is not dependent on the committee offering me this position. I don't have to make myself other than what I am in order to serve God."

Then she paused. Her voice lowered and slowed, as if she had suddenly dropped onto a comfortable sofa. Her next words came from a place deep inside. "I know that I am enough. This feels wonderful!"

Undoing Old Vows and Making New Ones

One day when Dave was six and walking alone by a railroad track, he made two vows, not that he knew what a vow was. That day something shifted in him that added up to a lifelong vow to himself, and he finally gave in to the despair he had been fighting since he was tiny. All his short life he had tried hard to get the love he so desperately needed. After that day on the railroad tracks, he stopped trying. Although he couldn't have articulated it then, he vowed, first of all, that he would never love anyone again. Second, never again would he let anyone love him.

At the time, his vows made a lot of sense, for his loveless childhood was full of devastating losses and rejection. Making these vows enabled him to insulate himself from searing pain and helped him survive as he grew up. After a time the actual vows were forgotten, but by then they had become a way of life.

At age forty he entered a Gestalt Pastoral Care growth process. He spoke of how relationships, especially with women, never worked out. He wept over his loneliness. A devout Christian, he very much desired to love others without deadening fear. As we worked together for many months, things did get better, but we both knew that he would need to take some deeper steps before he was free to love with joy and abandon.

One day the memory of walking along the railroad tracks surfaced, and with it Dave was able to name the vows he had made so long ago. He realized that his childhood vows had powerfully influenced his whole life. Together we decided to create a liturgy to renounce and undo his childhood vows and formally to take new faith-filled and life-giving vows.

The liturgy itself was very simple and was set in the context of a celebration of Eucharist with his Bible study group. At the appropriate time he told the story of the six-year-old who made vows on the railroad track, and how they helped him survive. He also told how these same vows later kept him from meaningful adult relationships. He was now trusting God through the prayers of this group to set him free.

Then Dave, with the help of the small congregation, formally turned away from that which had ruled his life:

> *Congregation:* Dave, when you were a child, you decided to never love again. Are you ready now to embrace a different way?

> *Dave:* Yes, I am, with God's help.

> *Congregation:* Dave, you also vowed to never again let another person love you. Are you ready to give up this vow and open yourself to the joys and risks of intimacy?

> *Dave:* Yes, I am, knowing that God's grace calls me forward.

As the Bible study group stood around him in a circle of support, Dave made his new vows:

> "My greatest desire is to love and be loved, and I firmly believe that God wants this for me. For my part, I promise to turn away from a way of death, and, as best I can, to embrace the life God gives me. I promise to pray for courage and discernment whenever I feel myself

shrink in fear from an opportunity for intimacy. I promise to trust that God will shape my life in ways that will bless me and others. Amen."

Then the congregation laid hands on him and prayed for the healing of his fear, and of the terrible experiences that had created the fear in the first place.

Although not dramatic on the outside, the results of this liturgy were immediately obvious to Dave. It was as if a door opened that enabled him to meet his crippling fears in a new way. It seemed God's grace was indeed at work, and slowly Dave's fears decreased. During this time the support of his Bible study group was crucial. Several months later he was able to point to his liturgy as a pivotal point in his growth. He is now happily married to a wonderful woman and has several children in whom he delights.[4]

Claiming Motherhood

At age fifteen Lucy gave up her infant son for adoption. She desperately wanted the child and considered keeping him but was wise enough to know that she was not ready to be a parent. Even so, during her pregnancy Lucy wrapped her heart around him like a blanket and knew that she would always be his secret and passionately loving mother. Though he would be named by his new parents, he would always be her own "Luke."

At the time she told few people about her loss, carrying her grief in private. She often thought of Luke, however, imagining him growing up and almost daily wondering what kind of person he was. Never did she stop loving him, and in her own mind, never did she stop being his mother. Each year, on Luke's birthday, she privately acknowledged the gift of his life and imagined what he might be doing at his age. For twenty-six years she held that secret, empty, and painful place in her heart open for him, as her only connection to his life.

When Luke was about to turn twenty-six, at the prompting of a friend, Lucy decided to ask for a liturgy to acknowledge publicly his important place in her life and her secret identity as his mother. She knew it was also time to let him go more deeply. Months before, she had contacted an agency that connects adult adopted children with their parents. At the time of the liturgy, Luke had not responded.

She invited some close friends and her therapist to be with her; I was there as pastor and worship leader. We met in a small United Methodist church in Brooklyn. Lucy's personal healing liturgy was set in the context of Eucharist, at the time for intercessory prayers.

During the liturgy, Lucy told the story of Luke's birth and shared publicly for the first time her painful decision to give him up for adoption. She told how she was advised to put the pregnancy behind her, forget about her son, and get on with her life. This she was unwilling to do. She recounted how she had kept a "Luke journal" for all these years, in which she wrote down poems, prayers, longings, and imaginings.

Twenty-six candles were on the altar, one for each year of Luke's life. As a friend lit each candle, Lucy read a letter to Luke, excerpted below, that recalled how she thought of him on each of his birthdays.

> When you were one, I wondered if your nose had straightened out and if you still looked like my brothers. I imagined you still having big brown eyes and thick black hair. I imagined talking infant babble with you . . .
>
> When you were two, I thought you must be impish.
>
> When you were three, I thought of you running and playing with Matchbox cars.
>
> . . . When you were nine, I thought you'd hate long division.
>
> . . . When you were thirteen, I wondered if you had kissed your first girl.
>
> . . . When you were seventeen, I wondered if I was a grandmother.
>
> . . . When you were twenty-three, I worried that you might have been injured in the Gulf War.
>
> . . . When you were twenty-four, I thought you must be a handsome man, working, making a living, maybe engaged or married.

. . . Now you are twenty-six. I want to know you, to hold you, to feel you, to know you are safe and happy and handsome, a good and godly man, strong in spirit.

When all the candles were lit, there was not a dry eye anywhere. I anointed Lucy, saying, "We in this congregation want to acknowledge the grief you have held secret for all these years. Together we declare that you are Luke's mother, because you have birthed and grieved and loved a child." Then we laid hands on her and prayed for the healing of the grief she had carried so long. We prayed for Luke and placed before God Lucy's yearning to find him.

When writing this book, I searched for Lucy to get her permission to tell her story. When I finally reached her by phone, she said, "Yes, of course, tell the story of my liturgy. But I just have to tell you that Luke and I have been in contact for ten years now. When he first called me, I sent a copy of the liturgy to him. He called back, sobbing. It was so healing for him. That liturgy was enormously healing for me too. I let go of so much that day. Luke is a wonderful man, and we see each other often. We are very close, sharing a splendid relationship. My life is so blessed!"

Liturgies of Surrender

⚜

Giving Up Family Shame and Sorrow

Jill came to an Opening to Grace workshop with a deep and familiar sorrow. She had long known that she was profoundly sad for the women who came before her: mother, grandmother, great-grandmother, great-great-grandmother, great-great-great-grandmother, and on back to the 1700s. She knew their names and some of their stories and loved them almost as if they were living friends. Some she called Dear Heart. It was as if her female ancestors had bequeathed to Jill their emotional DNA and were embedded in her body, emotions, and spirit in such a way that Jill was weeping their tears, feeling acutely their pain and shame, and somehow participating in their struggles. Recently Jill had had trouble breathing and still felt a sharp pain from her back to her chest, going through her heart. Doctors could find no medical reason for this pain. "I think my heart is broken for my mothers," Jill concluded.

Family stories convinced Jill that her valiant women ancestors had tried wholeheartedly to be good, even perfect, Christians. They had prayed much and read their Bibles often, worked hard at raising "good" children and kept their kitchens spotless, but they never really knew "the joy of the Lord." Most had suffered greatly from poverty, unremitting drudgery, and various profound losses. Some met far too early deaths.

Jill knew that this burden of family sorrow and shame was much too big for her. "I'm trying to be God with them, but how can I stop?" she said. "I so much want them to know that they didn't have to try so hard. All they had to do was trust that God loved them every minute of their imperfect lives." Then with a burst of understanding she said, "I think I've been trying somehow to heal all my mothers myself by carrying their burdens."

I invited her to ask Jesus what she should do about her mothers. She closed her eyes, and after a few minutes said, "Jesus is telling me to carry their burdens to him. Then my job will be done."

Jill's liturgical action was a simple one. On her lap she gathered throw pillows—one to represent each ancestor—until she was almost buried by the large pile. As the workshop group silently prayed for her, she spoke briefly to each woman, calling her by name and telling each that she didn't have to try so hard to be perfect, and that she was now giving her sorrow and shame to the Lord. Then Jill lovingly and solemnly laid each mother

We prayed that the seed just planted would grow large and would penetrate habits of thought, emotion, and spirit to help Jill learn to live in a new way.

at the feet of Jesus by physically placing the pillow bearing her name on the floor. With each surrender, Jill's breathing deepened, her physical heart pain lessened, and her face became more and more radiant. The ad hoc church witnessed this simple action and then laid hands on Jill and prayed that her healing process would continue. We prayed that the seed just planted would grow large and would penetrate habits of thought, emotion, and spirit to help Jill learn to live in a new way. We ended by singing a hymn, followed by each person telling Jill how we had been touched by her journey.

I spoke to Jill a few weeks later. She said, "It was as though a giant chunk of glass was pulled out of me at the retreat. Since then, a lot of smaller pieces have been falling out by themselves. I've noticed that when little 'opportunities for shame' come up, I can see them for what they are. They just evaporate because they have lost their emotional punch. It's really cool.

"And, by the way, I'm getting married in a few months. Carrying around the baggage of my female ancestors had kept me from freely going ahead with the marriage. Now I'm ready. Both of us are!"

Giving Up False Hope

Antonio had spent much of his life energy trying to get his father's approval. He had been a good boy, but his father never even granted him a special smile. He got excellent grades in high school and college in the hope his father would say, "Good job!" He became a doctor and then a sought-after surgeon, hoping that his father would finally say, "Antonio, I am so proud of you." His father never varied in his responses; either he excoriated Antonio for his shortcomings or warned him that accomplishing so much would give him "the bighead," and that then Antonio would be "too good" for his family. His father died never having given Antonio the slightest glimmer of approval.

Although Antonio liked his work, loved his wife and kids, and outwardly was happy, his father's disapproval snaked through his live like a sludgy river. Although after a time Antonio seldom thought about his father, he still was bent on accomplishing more and more, and amassing the signs of success: big houses and cars, expensive vacations, gourmet food and fine wines. Obsessively chasing success had become a way of life.

In his spiritual life, Antonio's mode of operation was the same; he set out to become a spiritual success. He gave large sums to charity and sometimes waived his fee for patients who could not pay for his services. He played with his kids regularly and was sweet to his wife. He sought to do everything just right. Even though Antonio knew better, he was desperately trying to earn his way into God's love, just as he had sought his father's.

When Antonio came to an Opening to Grace retreat, he was tired of the way he had been living; tired of doing everything just right; and, despite his accomplishments, tired of never feeling good enough. He had been in psychotherapy for some time and knew that, against all sense and reason, he still was trying to please his father, who had been dead for ten years. I suggested that he pray with faith imagination and tell this to Jesus. As Antonio closed his eyes, he pictured Jesus sitting directly in front of him, smiling slightly. Antonio repeated to Jesus just what he had told the group. Then Jesus spoke, and Antonio heard in his "mind's ear": "Antonio, I approve of you, and I'm so proud of you. You don't have to earn my love. You don't have to prove how successful you are. I love you."

Antonio burst into tears. He wept and wept—the tears of a small boy, a teenager, a young doctor, and a middle-aged big shot. As the ad hoc church prayed silently for him, he cried the tears of a lifetime, healing and transforming tears. When he was finished, I asked if he would see what Jesus wanted him to do with the false hope that his father would ever come through for him. The answer was immediate. "Jesus wants me to give my false hope to him. He wants me to let my hope come from God."

Solemnly he picked up a large, heavy sofa cushion. "This is my false hope," he said, "and I'm taking it to the chapel." We followed him out the door and into the tiny chapel. He placed his false hope on the altar, saying, "Okay, God. You've got it. Show me how to trust you instead of my ability to succeed." With his permission the ad hoc church gathered around him in the crowded chapel and prayed that

When Antonio came to an Opening to Grace retreat, he was tired of the way he had been living; tired of doing everything just right; and despite his accomplishments, tired of never feeling good enough.

God would plant this movement of growth into him more deeply. They prayed that Antonio learn how to live without chasing success or its trappings. They prayed in thanksgiving for the healing that had already begun.

The end of Antonio's simple liturgy came later in the day when Antonio said, "I want you to know that I feel wonderful. Such a burden has been lifted. This is really amazing. I know something really happened, because I could never have allowed myself to look so unsuccessful as to cry like that in front of you people. You should congratulate me on my new 'unsuccess.'"

We were glad to do so.

Liturgies of Grieving

A Funeral, One Year Later

Sakhile was a lonely African student in the United States, struggling to get an advanced degree. Passionate about returning to help the people of his impoverished country, Sakhile frugally subsisted on a pittance and poured his energy into hard study. Halfway through his academic program, disaster crashed into his life; quite suddenly his beloved mother died back home. The funeral was to be in his African hometown, with all his relatives in attendance. Sakhile was painfully torn between returning home or staying in the States. Going to his mother's funeral would mean an end to his studies; he could not afford the enormous cost of extra airfare to return to the USA. Finally he decided he must stay put, even though to him it was an insult to his mother's memory, almost like another death.

The price of this decision was tremendous. Sakhile couldn't really share his grieving with his family, even by phone; expensive, rushed phone calls just didn't do it. Neither could he convey to his American friends how devastated he was, and so he simply returned to his classes with tears shed in private and a large hole torn in his heart. His mother's death was not marked in America in any way.

Fast-forward to ten months later. Hearing of Sakhile's great loss, a small group of church friends, along with his pastor, offered to plan a funeral with him. They spent many hours with him, hearing stories about his mother and the funeral customs at home in Africa. They asked about his mother's favorite hymns and what scriptures had been read at her funeral. They enlarged a picture of his mother to use as a focal point during the memorial service. Someone found a hand-woven fabric from the student's country and made an altar cloth with it. Another made a CD of music that might have been part of his mother's funeral, and Sakhile contributed a wooden cross from home to place on the altar. On the anniversary of his mother's death, they had a funeral as similar as possible to the one at home, and Sakhile was able at last to cry in the community of faith and begin his mourning in earnest. He was warmed and grateful for the big effort on his behalf by his American church.

Obviously, such exquisitely loving care calls on the ministry of the laity in a major way, requiring generous time and commitment; however, I have come to expect that the ad hoc congregation at a personalized liturgy will also be greatly blessed. Those participating with Sakhile were amazed by the liturgy's effect on him and felt honored to be a part of it. They loved being engaged in genuine ministry. And they themselves were challenged to explore their own needs for grief work. As I have come to expect, Sakhile's liturgy benefited everyone present.

Creating a Memorial Shrine

Suzette, a beautiful young woman, flew to New York City dazed, grieving, traumatized, and utterly alone. Just months before, she had barely escaped with her life from the terrible slaughter in her native Rwanda between the warring Hutu and Tutsi tribes. Her miraculous rescue by a human rights organization was an amazing and compelling story in itself, but haunting Suzette's days and nights was the devastating knowledge that while she had escaped, every member of her family in Rwanda had been killed. Mother, father, siblings, aunts, uncles, cousins—all dead. Friends, acquaintances, work associates, fellow students—also murdered.

Such trauma is beyond the experience or comprehension of most of us. As best I could, I listened to Suzette's stories, held her when she wept, and prayed with her when the horrifying memories and terror slammed into her again and again. About a year into this process, she was able to clarify what she needed so she could go ahead with her grief and, ultimately, her life: "I need for all these dead people to be recognized! I need for their names to be known and for there to be a place where I can go to remember them. I need for someone besides me to know that I loved them and that I love them still." Then followed a fresh geyser of tears, for none of her Rwandan family and friends had had a funeral or even an individual burial place.

I felt she was absolutely right in wanting recognition for her dear ones, and that her longing for such a liturgy was evidence of much healing already. At my suggestion we decided to create a special place of remembrance and hold a funeral there for all her dead. Some other people besides Suzette would then be able to carry the knowledge that these people had lived, loved, struggled, and died as victims of violence and hatred. Together we could proclaim that the cruel deaths were not the end; her family was alive in God.

Amazed that we could really do this, Suzette grew more eager as we laid our plans. With her permission I contacted The Prayer House Community, of which I am a member, to help us. Our small ecumenical group meets four weekends a year to administer and care for a tiny hermitage for solitary prayer in the Pocono Mountains, and to support one another's ministries. The group was glad to help create the memorial on our bit of land and to be the congregation for the funeral service. Since Suzette is a Roman Catholic, as were most of the dead, Father Peter, a member of our community, volunteered to preside at a Mass at the memorial. Bette Sohm, a friend who is an experienced creator of both stage sets and worship settings, agreed to make a preliminary design of the memorial and help us with some of the technical problems.

So it was that early one July Saturday, ten of us gathered with

Suzette at The Prayer House to construct the memorial. We began with prayer that the Holy Spirit would lead us in what we were about to do, and we asked that the creation of the memorial be healing for Suzette. Suzette prayed in her African way that the memorial would please her ancestors and put them to rest.

Then we got to work. It was important to Suzette that each person's name be permanently recorded at the memorial. At Bette's suggestion, we had begged a large cache of polished granite scraps from a Staten Island company that manufactures kitchen countertops. Bette brought some small drill-like etching tools to carve the names of Suzette's dead friends and relatives, one to a stone. None of us had ever tried to write on granite before, but by the day's end we had succeeded in carving readable names of Suzette's family and friends: Mutoni, Pascal, Louise, Kamondo, Adele, Jean Pierre, Alfred, Simbizi, seventy-nine names in all. We placed the remaining blank granite pieces in a container, along with a permanent marking pen, so that visitors to the memorial could write names of other victims of violence around the world. On the largest piece of granite we wrote:

> In memory of the one million people
> whose lives were taken by genocide:
> Rwanda, 1990–1994.
> Pray that God may heal the scars of war
> and empower humankind
> to embrace justice and peace.

Meanwhile, some of us were clearing a little area of land to create an open space for the memorial itself. Although Bette had a drawing of the shape the memorial might take, that day we seemed simply to follow our instincts. We found ourselves piling up a long mound of earth and placing dug-up pieces of slate on the top and sides of the mound. While all this was going on, Suzette moved between the etchers and the earthmovers, making suggestions, pitching in, and mostly telling us stories about the various people who would be memorialized there. Standing back some hours later, we realized that without really planning to, we had made an altar. Someone had made a beautiful wooden cross, and this we attached to a tree behind the mound. Finally, we put the name-stones on the altar.

Suzette stared at our creation for a few moments, then said with unusual intensity, "What this altar needs is some color! What do we have around here that has color?" We quickly found some broken pieces of stained glass that "just happened" to be in the shed, and Suzette glued them to the slate all over the altar, transforming its top and sides into a vivid collage. She also created a beautiful stained-glass mosaic on the cross. "There! *Now* it's done," she declared. Clearly she was not only referring to our physical work at that moment, but also to an important stage of her grief process. A crucial leg of her journey had indeed been completed.

After much-needed showers, the community gathered early in the evening for the memorial Mass. Tea lights were lit and placed on the altar and into the surrounding woods. Peter and Suzette sat down together on a small bench in front facing the rest of us. As Peter later said, at that moment he had a strong and surprising impression that in a profoundly spiritual sense, it was as if Suzette was copresiding with him at the memorial Eucharist. She had needed it, asked for it, and helped plan it. Although the Mass belongs to the whole church, this was her service, uniquely shaped to touch her experience and pain, and to proclaim that even in Rwanda, death has been overcome.

During the Mass each name was read, and a gong was rung for each person, followed by a short silence. We commended each person to God's care, trusting in God's mercy and love to receive that soul. We also prayed for the murderers and their families and for the end of hatred and violence in Rwanda. Together we shared Eucharist with the awareness that, in God's mystery, we also shared it with those who had died.

The Eucharist was deeply meaningful for all of us, gathering up as it did all the work we had done that day. We were well aware that the liturgy really began in the morning with our prayer that God would bless our efforts. As we shoveled and etched and hauled rocks and listened to Suzette's stories, elements of liturgy were obviously present in our focused interior prayers: praise for God's redeeming presence in the presence of evil, thanksgiving for "this treasure in earthen vessels" (2 Cor. 4:7, KJV), confession of our own complicity with violence and hatred, intercession for Suzette and for the world, proclamation of our family relationship with all people, and the declaration in stone of God's love, which nothing can destroy. The Mass gave our liturgy of work a more formal and explicit expression.

After dinner Suzette tried to teach her clumsy, and by now exquisitely tired, American friends to dance to a drumbeat, African-style. Again and again she showed us how to move our bodies in that sinuous and rhythmic way that came so easily to her. We never did get it, but we had a wonderfully goofy time trying, and the evening ended with much hilarity and blowing off steam. Suzette loved this impromptu fun and later said that it was a "very African response to a funeral." That night was the first time I had ever seen her laugh heartily or, for that matter, express any sort of pleasure.

This special liturgy did not end Suzette's pain and grief. She had much more inner work to do, but on that day a noticeable shift occurred in her. She, who had felt so alone and frightened in her new country, was greatly moved to be surrounded by a group of people who had gathered to "be church" for her. She appreciated being with a community again, something she had missed greatly since leaving Africa. She later reported that she was finding it easier to trust others. She was emphatic that our interest in listening to the names and stories of her Rwandan past was deeply meaningful and important to her. The name-stones and the place of memory were crucial too, comforting her and helping her say good-bye more fully. As she had said, she needed a place that would function as a cemetery. A year later Suzette commented that the memorial remained an important milestone in her healing. "Just having the memorial there," she said, "makes me feel better about the world." The funeral Mass itself was vital; it assured her heart that her dear ones were indeed with God.

It was as if her chest and heart opened up that day, literally allowing her to breathe easier.

Although the day was planned to meet Suzette's needs, she was not the only one blessed; the process also personally enriched and moved the gathered community. It was important for us to identify with the suffering of the world and to participate in its healing. We loved the chance to be church for Suzette, and we recognized what a privilege it was to be used for the healing of another. As a member of The Prayer House Community put it, "Our lives and prayer have been deeply affected by this experience. Our ministry feels more connected with the pain of our sisters and brothers, and our faith in the power of God's grace has grown stronger because of our journey with Suzette."

The memorial shrine continues to be a place of memory, tears, and hope for those who spend time at The Prayer House. People still write names on granite pieces and place them at the altar. Some stop to pray for victims of new violence that has erupted since we created the memorial. Others come to Suzette's memorial to declare their faith that "the light shines in the darkness, and the darkness did not overcome it" (John 1:5).

Liturgies in Desolation

Losing a Job, Gaining Hope

Manuel always considered himself incredibly blessed that he got paid for creating beautiful, functional, custom-made wood furniture. At age fifty-five this respected and sought-after master craftsman was suddenly let go from the company he had been with since he was an apprentice. Understandably, he was depressed and devastated, and his depression did not improve as months went by without his finding a new job.

As Manuel spoke with his pastor about his situation, his pastor was immediately drawn to the idea of holding a special liturgy to pray for Manuel. Manuel was a bit nonplussed at first but soon warmed to his pastor's suggestion. As they talked it over, Manuel saw that he needed to admit the ways he was partly at fault for losing his job—his chronic lateness and his rigidity about "doing things right," which kept him from adjusting easily to customers' requests. He also wanted God to touch his depression and show him the way forward.

In planning the liturgy it was clear to his pastor that Manuel's deepest inner language involved creating with his hands rather than making vows or theological statements. He was thoroughly a hands-on kind of guy, especially when it came to wood. Accordingly, Manuel and his pastor decided that Manuel would invite a small group of church friends to his home, where he had a small carpentry shop in his basement. After telling the story of his job loss and subsequent depression, Manuel would take a beautiful piece of lumber and ceremonially split it in half lengthwise to acknowledge that he had been ripped apart by the loss of his job. Under Manuel's direction, the group would carefully and prayerfully help him sand and polish the two pieces of wood. Manuel would then attach the two pieces to form a cross, which would be hung on the wall of Manuel's workshop.

Then the ad hoc church would anoint Manuel and, putting their hands on him, pray for his healing and for a new job. The simple service went as planned, with a few members of Manuel's church in attendance, honored to be there. Even though Manuel's outward situation had not changed, by the end of the service Manuel was feeling more hopeful and profoundly thankful for the support of the ad hoc church.

In the weeks that followed, Manuel felt lighter, stronger, and more self-confident every time he looked at the cross in his basement; soon he resumed his job search with renewed vigor. Whether or not he found a new job, Manuel was clear that he would always be a carpenter, and that his life was in God's hands. Losing his job didn't seem like such a tragedy; after all, a lifetime of thrift and good investments meant that he didn't really need the money.

Before long he did, in fact, get a new carpentry job similar to his old one.

Creating a Garden of Hope

Julia lost both her children in a terrible automobile accident, and she herself was badly injured. Eight months later her husband, who had been driving the car, left her. After working with a physical therapist, a psychotherapist, and a spiritual director for nearly two years, she was still devastated. Her old life was gone, and in its place was an existence consisting of constant pain and loss that invaded every part of her.

Julia tried to cling to the faith that had meant so much before the accident, but it was as if she was spiritually dead. She could not pray, could not sense God's presence, could not find comfort in scripture. She could, however, remember times in her old life when she had been healed and prodded to grow by Christ, and she wanted to believe that healing was still possible for her. Since she had not been able to pray for many months, she and her spiritual director thought maybe she could create a "physical prayer," a sign of her desire for renewed faith and of God's desire to redeem and make things new.

Because Julia had always loved flowers, she decided that her physical prayer would take the form of a flower garden—even though she was still flattened by pain and didn't feel at all flowery. Her garden, to be planted in a trash-filled and desolate vacant lot across the street from her house, would be a sign that she was embracing God's promise of hope and new life—even in stark desolation.

Julia and five good friends, along with her spiritual director, met early one morning for her special garden-making liturgy. They began with a hymn and a prayer that their actions would be healing for Julia and that they would be attentive to the meaning of what they were doing. The group agreed not to engage in small talk during the day; rather, they would speak briefly of what they were feeling, share the meanings they discerned in their physical work together, and pray for Julia from time to time. Julia deeply desired the prayers and words of her friends, but she didn't feel ready yet to form verbal prayers herself. She asked her friends to supply the words; she was doing the best she could just by being there to work.

At each stage of the project, the group paused often to pray for Julia. Occasional comments from the spiritual director helped them remember that the weedy vacant lot was a metaphor for Julia's suffering, and the garden was a sign of God's work in her.

As the debris was picked up and hauled away, Julia's friends prayed that God would clear away any pain she was finished with, any baggage she no longer needed. They asked that God lay bare anything in Julia that was hard-packed and neglected and that her painful places would be exposed to God's softening, cleansing, and healing. As the group dug up the soil, they prayed for God to prepare the way for new growth in Julia, for God to "turn things over" and break up her inner clods and clots. While spreading fertilizer, they asked God to enrich Julia's soul again and give her what she needed to grow. As they planted seeds and set out seedlings, they asked God to plant a new heart in Julia, to give her seeds of hope and renewed faith. When they watered the thirsty ground, they asked that the living water of Christ rain down on Julia and heal her in body, mind, and spirit. One friend gave Julia a stone etched with the word *hope*. The friend laid the stone in the garden while saying these words:

> "Julia, in the name of the God who loves you, in the name of Jesus who heals you, in the name of the Holy Spirit who is with you even when you have no awareness of Presence, we lay this stone in your special garden. We put it here as a shorthand reminder of the whole gospel, and of what we have done here today. We put it here in the faith that your children are with God, and that God will meet you in your inner desolation. We urge you to come often to this sacred space as a way of praying. We put this stone here as a sign of our own love for you, and our willingness to support you when you need us. Amen."

When their work was finished, the friends anointed Julia in the new garden and affirmed their own faith that God had always been with her and would continue to be with her as she healed. Then they surrounded Julia, and putting their garden-grimy hands on her head, prayed in silence as she wept familiar tears of grief, but now mingled with hope and gratitude.

As the plants grew and began to bloom, Julia found increasing comfort in the garden. These were not just any flowers; through the simple liturgy that had blessed them, these flowers had become living symbols of hope and promise. It almost seemed that the flowers were praying *for* her when Julia herself could not yet pray, and sometimes even praying *with* her as she offered her jumbled feelings and pain to the Lord. Indeed it seemed that God was speaking to Julia, and for Julia, at a time when she could not muster the energy herself. The neighbors noticed the garden, of course, and began stopping by. As Julia told how the garden had come to be planted, folks shared some of their own stories of loss with her. Julia found herself listening and praying with them. She began to enjoy bringing a thermos of lemonade to share whenever she was in the garden, and friendships began to sprout along with the flowers. Other neighbors dropped in to help weed and water, occasionally adding new plants. One contributed a lovely bench. As the garden became more and more of a community project, Julia felt herself slowly coming alive again. She said, "The liturgy opened the door for me, and every time I come to the garden, the liturgy sort of continues. I guess it's [shown me] that God's work continues in me and has even spread to my neighborhood. That's amazing! I could never have dreamed that my pain would help someone else. I still have my down days, but I can't begin to tell you how much I've shifted toward joy."

Liturgies of Healing from Sexual Abuse

Telling a Secret

Amelia, a faithful and dedicated pastor, came to an Opening to Grace workshop with a shame-filled secret. Her ex-husband was also a pastor and, she had discovered, an active pedophile. When Amelia first found out that he had molested children in several churches over a period of years, she was horrified and paralyzed. She could scarcely let this awful discovery enter her mind, and for weeks she was in a sort of shocked daze in which she repeated over and over to herself, "I just can't believe it." She finally managed to leave with her children and began the process of divorce, but it was several years before she could bring herself to blow the whistle that sent her husband to jail. In the meantime—and here is where her guilt was overwhelming—her husband was still molesting children.

After making a new start in a different state, Amelia vowed to never again speak of her terrible secret. With the tenacity of the survivor she is, she tightly locked up her past, and most of the time she didn't even think about it. Her children and her ministry were the center of her life, and she found great fulfillment as a loving mother and a sensitive pastor. Her secret was still there, though, slowly growing tentacles that occasionally broke through her happiness. When she was with friends or parishioners she would sometimes think, *If they knew, they would reject me.* The next thought was usually, *I can't tell my terrible story to anyone!* She made sure she didn't stay with any church for long; she moved before people could get very close to her.

Matters came to a head when preaching became difficult; sometimes she just couldn't find the words. Although she continued to feel a strong call to ministry, frequently she didn't feel worthy to administer the sacraments. Wisely, at this point she sought help, and her counselor, to whom she choked out her secret, became a lifeline of support.

After many sessions, together they decided it might be time for Amelia to break the power of her shame by revealing her past to some trusted listeners. Amelia prayed that if the Opening to Grace retreat was the right place to tell her secret, God would give her a clear sign. To her great surprise, there were three "signs" in the form of three other workshop participants (in a group of six) who had had experiences that directly touched the core issue of Amelia's secret. One of the three told her own story of a pedophile husband, a story that was practically identical to Amelia's.

The retreat group didn't set out to create a liturgy for Amelia; one simply emerged spontaneously. It began with Amelia letting her carefully guarded barriers fall as she told her secret. She ended with a bravely direct question for the group: "I need to know. Do you reject me now?" The participants responded tenderly, compassionately, and honestly that they felt honored to be there, that what they felt most was God's love for her, that they felt the room filled with God's presence, and that they had a sense of worship and awe as soon as she began.

The leader, sensing a rare opportunity, framed the experience by saying: "I think we have been ushered into the beginning of a special healing service for Amelia. I suggest, if it is okay with you, Amelia, that we respond to you liturgically as well as personally. Would it be all right with you if each of us said to you, 'Amelia, "neither do I condemn you"' and then add a formal declaration of forgiveness for not calling the police sooner?"

Amelia nodded, and members of the ad hoc church gathered around her, saying:

"Amelia, we remember how Jesus said to the woman, 'neither do I condemn you.'" I say it too. Neither do I condemn you. In the name of Jesus, I know you are forgiven for not calling the police sooner, because you confessed it with repentance. You have been repenting for years and years. Now it's time to enter into the joy of the Lord!

"Amelia, neither do I condemn you. In the name of Jesus, I tell you that there is no condemnation in Christ.

"Amelia, neither do I condemn you. As a sinner myself, I know that the good news of Jesus Christ says that you don't have to carry guilt around."

By now Amelia was breathing heavily, drinking in their words. Then she gasped, "I need to feel clean! I need to feel clean!" With Amelia's permission, the group got a bowl of water, asked God to bless it, and "splashed her with cleansing grace" as they proclaimed:

"Amelia, by the power of the Holy Spirit you are cleansed from the terrible experience with your husband.

"Amelia, in the name of Jesus Christ, we wash you clean of shame.

"Amelia, we break the power of the voice you heard inside, saying, 'Don't tell! Don't tell!' With this water we remind you that the truth will set you free.

"Amelia, with this water, in the name of Jesus, we dissolve the connection between you and your husband's actions."

At one point a participant in the ad hoc church poured some of the water into a Communion chalice and said:

"Amelia, drink this water, and let God's grace cleanse your insides from guilt and shame."

The brief liturgy ended with laying on of hands, prayer for her continued healing, and sharing of reactions. The group sent her home with the remaining water in a small bottle, suggesting that she pour it into her bath sometime when she could "soak in grace" even more deeply.

Several days later, Amelia said in an e-mail to her ad hoc church:

> I feel like I've made a major shift in my perspective on my divorce story—the liturgy of cleansing was so powerful and has put me in a whole new place. I know there may still be struggles, but I'll never go back to where I was. (I know you were trying to be cautious with the amount of water, but I wouldn't have minded if you'd poured it over my head!) . . . [When I was handed the chalice full of water] I can't tell you what a holy moment that was . . . it was one of the most sacred things I have ever experienced. . . . It symbolized for me the cleansing of my life in the church—my work as a pastor and preacher, and it healed those hurts and feelings of unworthiness. It broke the spell of poison. . . . There has been a massive shift from fear/panic/shame, and sometimes even terror—to peace, cleanliness, and acceptance. . . . Thanks so much for the prayers, for the washing, for the friendship, for the sharing, for letting God use you. . . . It's like a spell has been broken. I hold you all in prayer and close to my heart. May God's Spirit enrich your lives as only God can do.

On the one-year anniversary of her impromptu liturgy, Amelia wrote to say that the effects of the liturgy still "held," to the great surprise of her counselor.

Pablo's Confession

At an Opening to Grace retreat many years ago, by coincidence five participants were women who had been sexually abused as children by important men in their lives. Two other women were there as observers/intercessors. The other participant was Pablo, a compassionate, sensitive, and prayerful man. At first the women were more than a little distressed to have Pablo present in a setting where each had hoped to work with her abuse experiences. They found it emotionally difficult to trust him, though they recognized rationally that he was no threat at all. In this group of wounded persons, it was clear that Pablo, a gentle and caring man, bore the stigma of being male, and thus was a potential victimizer.

Pablo did not get defensive; instead he offered to leave the room immediately if any woman requested he do so. He said he would gladly go into the chapel and pray for everyone; he didn't want to be a scary problem that might stand in the way of healing. Pablo's willingness not to intrude was a veritable tonic for the women. Several times they asked him to go into the next room briefly and then come back, only to be ordered away again, just to experience what it was like to have a man respect their boundaries. Eager to help any way he could, Pablo went along with this little exercise. Finally, with growing trust, each woman asked him to stay with the group as she did her inner work.

As the stories unfolded, each woman's story was alike in one detail: the adult male abusers had insisted that they had done nothing wrong. Each woman lamented how painful was this denial. "If only he would admit it or give me some feeling that he was willing to face up to what he did, it would be so much easier to go on with my life," one woman wept.

When the time came for Pablo's own inner work, he said that he had wondered at first what in the world he was doing in this group. Maybe he shouldn't have come, he thought, but perhaps God had a special purpose in his being here. Then Pablo described how, as he witnessed the women's intense work, he felt an urgency take shape inside. Just as he had represented abusive males for a time in the group, he now wanted to represent males who are appalled at abusive behavior and who feel compassionate toward suffering abuse survivors.

Pablo then blurted out a question: could he confess on behalf of the women's abusers? He didn't quite know what he was doing or why; he just felt pushed to confess for "those who didn't know to do it for themselves." All of us, including Pablo himself, were a bit stunned at his request, but it seemed just right. So, Pablo began an amazing liturgical action that took us all into the presence of grace at work. Kneeling and weeping, he confessed to God the damage done to little girls by abusive males. For a few minutes it was if he was an Israelite priest confessing the corporate sins of the people.

Soon, however, Pablo realized that he was not just making a second-hand confession; he was surprised to find that he had one of his own to make. Although he hadn't thought about it for years, as an eight-year-old he had once hit a seven-year-old girl and pulled down her panties for a few seconds in their subsequent scuffle. The girl finally socked him hard and ran away. Right away he felt bad about what he had done and told no one about it. As he grew up, he filed this experience—accurately—under "childish mistakes," knowing that many children do such things. Although this incident was the only time he ever physically hurt anyone, being with the women had helped him realize two things: that the girl might have suffered more than he thought and that despite his gentleness, he was capable, like most of us, of cruelty. As Pablo came to know himself better, he felt a weight he hadn't been aware of carrying slide off his shoulders.

Pablo's liturgical action was healing for everyone. The women heard his story with compassion and much gratitude. Every one of them said that Pablo's spontaneous liturgical action had helped them enormously in letting go of painful memories. One said, "I think I was holding on to the pain of my sexual abuse as a way of holding on to the truth of what happened. Having Pablo acknowledge and admit male guilt has given me a new freedom to let go of the pain."

Tough Love

Bob, a committed Christian and still single in middle age, was at a low point of confusion and depression about his life when he began toying with Internet child pornography. The new habit quickly ballooned into a secret and shame-filled addiction, and inevitably he moved beyond pictures to desire for the actual experience. One day he traveled to a distant location to meet someone (actually a detective) from a favorite Internet site, who promised to take him somewhere to "play." The encounter resulted in Bob's arrest, with charges of soliciting sex with minors and statutory rape. A trial date was set, and he was released on bail.

News of his arrest traveled quickly in his small-town, closely knit church community. Members were torn between anger, shock, dismay, fear for their children, and a genuine desire to be faithful and loving. Bob immediately wrote a letter to the church, expressing his humiliation, guilt, and sorrow for betraying them and his own faith.

The members, many of whom were parents of young children, decided to ban Bob temporarily from all church activities. Nevertheless, the church felt a sacred responsibility to support one of their own who was in trouble, and with amazing "tough love," they set up a special committee, an accountability and support group to work with him. Bob's church community was like family to him, and he was pleased to agree.

Bob's support group invited parents in the congregation to express their grave concerns to them and to Bob. Others came to vent their outrage. Some spoke of how they liked Bob and how shocked they felt by his actions. Still others remembered that Bob had survived a terrible and victimized childhood and that there were explainable reasons for his behavior. A few pointed out that although he might have abused a child face-to-face, he had not actually done it. No one, however, was willing to brush off the seriousness of his crime. At the same time they reminded one another often of the gospel imperative to work for reconciliation and healing. For months these intense reactions were respectfully heard, acknowledged, and accepted by the accountability and support group; Bob listened and responded as well. Next the committee invited trained mediators to work with the congregation to help deal creatively with these surging emotional and spiritual currents. Their goal was to support Bob while holding his feet to the fire and to work toward healing. Bob explained, "The support group was so meaningful to me. I knew I needed them in order to get past this, and their support meant the world. I appreciated so much that the committee did not just vent anger, nor did they just want to make me feel better. I wanted them to ask tough questions, and they did. I know that sugarcoating won't help anything. I have to go to these dark places, although I'm not looking forward to it."

Out of the mediation process emerged a concrete plan to welcome Bob back into the full life of the church. The accountability and support group formulated some conditions Bob would have to fulfill for as long as they deemed necessary, which included repentance of his sin and certain positive steps to face his addiction.

Before Bob could return, the support group stipulated that he would have to agree to therapy with a sex offender specialist. He had to continue to cooperate with the accountability and support group and meet with it regularly. He must be constantly and closely accompanied by a group member every second he was on church property. Above all, he was to have absolutely no contact with children anywhere. For its part, the church would actively support and pray for Bob in his healing, and would be present for him at the court hearing and trial.

Bob agreed to these terms, and it was decided that when the accountability and support group felt Bob was ready, there would be a congregational liturgy to lift up what God had accomplished already among them. In the liturgy they would strive to recognize everyone's emotional reactions, set forth Bob's special covenant with the church, proclaim the gospel of forgiveness and mercy, and pray for healing. Bob would then be anointed, hands would be laid on him as people prayed for healing, and he would be formally welcomed back into the church.

The extraordinary liturgy was written by a seminary graduate, with much input from a mature, steady laywoman. (In this instance, the recipient didn't have much to do with specific planning, although he agreed ahead of time to the general contours the service would take.) Although worship in their church usually is fairly relaxed, they decided to make Bob's liturgy tightly structured to minimize the possibility of spontaneous distractions or speeches. The committee would continue to invite the sharing and working through of feelings and conflicts at other times, but in this liturgy they would express their shared commitment to being a healing church. Bob would be given a copy of the liturgy ahead of time so he could prepare his heart to respond with honesty.

On the day of the service, Bob was anxious and worried. Although he knew that his church was not likely to subject him to public excoriation, he felt that "they were fully within their rights to do so." His guilt was enormous and appropriate.

The liturgy began with a hymn and a reading of Romans 8:38-39, followed by a prayer. To set the context, someone summarized the congregation's journey with Bob, and the accountability and support group gave an update on their work.

During the sermon the pastor shared a compelling image of church. He said that when a robin builds her nest, it is made from broken sticks and the mother's own feathers, and one more very special ingredient. "Holding it all together like mortar," he said, "is dried bird poop." Amazingly, he went on, a fragile shelter made of sacrifice, brokenness, and bodily waste makes a perfect environment to nurture the tiny birds. Our poop—our sin and brokenness—surrounded by the feathers of God's love is what holds us together as a church. In fact, poop offers extraordinary opportunities for healing and growth.

Following this story, lemon wedges were passed out with an invitation to "taste the sourness of life" and to reflect on "when we have hurt or been hurt." Tiny cups of honey followed for the congregation to "taste the sweetness of hope and grace."

The heart of the service was a series of questions asked of Bob. He was in tears for much of the remainder of the service.

> *Church:* Bob, we, your faith community, are gathered here this evening with you to mark the next step in the process of restoration and healing for all concerned. We deeply regret your choices. We understand that you, too, regret your behavior and feel remorse and pain because of it.

Bob: Yes, that is correct.

Church: Bob, it is our understanding that deep and harmful patterns of thinking and behavior that come out of your human brokenness led to your being willing to carry out abusive behavior.

Bob: Yes, I agree.

Church: Bob, we believe that you will benefit from specific professional help so that you can begin to address these issues. It is our hope that you willingly choose to walk through the hard journey that is needed in order to change the patterns of thinking that allowed you to be willing to engage in abusive behavior, and that you will hang in there despite the pain that you will need to face on that journey.

Bob: Yes, this is my hope and my commitment.

Church: Bob, we, your faith community, commit to walk with you in love as we support you and hold you accountable on the next steps of that journey.

Bob: I welcome your support and your commitment to hold me accountable.

Church: Bob, our willingness to walk with you in love comes out of our love and care for you as a person, out of our knowledge that you will need both support and accountability, out of our acknowledgment that you are part of the body of Christ, out of our desire for your healing so that you can share your gifts with us, and out of our belief that this is an opportunity for us to share God's healing love with you. We are also anxious for your healing because we want to do what we can to make sure there are never any victims.

Bob: I welcome your support.

Church: Bob, we carry a deep concern for victims of abuse, and we are concerned about and committed to making sure our children are safe and that they feel safe. For this reason we choose to establish the following guidelines for your interaction with our children:

1. You cannot be alone with our children at any time.

2. When at church, you will need to be accompanied by a designated person until such time that your accountability and support group decides otherwise.

Bob: I accept these limitations.

Bob was then surrounded by his church friends, who anointed him and prayed for his healing. He was then invited to sign the special covenant of the church that all members renew yearly. With that, he was welcomed back into the activities and services of the church.

A final prayer of thanksgiving expressed the strong and gritty faith of this courageous church:

Thanks be to God, who loves and restores us;
who makes us like a watered garden,
a spring of water, whose waters never fail;
who grants us the love, power, and grace to find healing for the past,
and wisdom and grace for the future. Amen.

As this book is being written, Bob will soon begin serving a two- to four-year sentence in a special prison for sex offenders. For him the hardest part is not going to prison but knowing "I betrayed my own values. I betrayed the relationships with my friends and family and church. That's awful to face and admit." Even so, he expects his church will continue to support him through letters and visits. He knows his healing has just begun, but already he treasures the honesty and support his church gave him, especially at his special service. Months after the service he commented, "I could hardly get through it. All I could do was weep and choke out those responses. It was beautiful, and it was hard to hear. It was genuine. It was the church taking me seriously, and not cheap grace. I liked how it fully acknowledged my crime, my repentance, God's grace, and my own responsibility to do something with it."

Bob is right. Now it is his responsibility to walk the scary, difficult, terrifyingly honest and grace-filled path ahead.

Eileen's Cleansing

Eileen, a Roman Catholic nun, was raped repeatedly by her father for most of her childhood. With each rape he told his confused and frightened daughter that he knew what was best for her. He loved her, he said, and wanted to teach her how to love too. As Eileen entered puberty, the abuse continued unabated. Her father became ferocious about keeping her away from boys her own age because, as he said, her body belonged to him. According to his twisted thinking, there was a special bond between father and daughter that he couldn't allow anyone else to "violate." He threatened that if she ever told anyone "their secret," she would really be sorry.

Sexual abuse thrives on family denial. Eileen's mother acted as if nothing was wrong; in fact she spent much energy showing the world that she was the mom of an ideal family. She had dissociated, that is, she put the obvious signs of Eileen's abuse behind a locked door of her awareness and pretended everything was just peachy.

After years of threats, indoctrination, fear, and isolation, Eileen felt numb inside. By then she had learned to dissociate just like her mother. Whenever her father was near, Eileen would simply go somewhere else in her head, leaving her body behind for him to use. She had been effectively robbed of inner resources and energy to reach out to anyone who might have offered help.

Eileen left home as soon as she could, but moving out did not end her pain. In a sense her father came with her, for although the overt incest had ended, now he was ensconced in her body, emotions, and spirit. The memory of his abuse still controlled her reactions, drew strict boundaries between her and others, and whispered into her soul that no one but he could possibly love her. Finally, at age twenty-eight she began to work on the trauma of her childhood abuse.

After a year Eileen had made a great deal of progress. She was able to name her experience as abusive and wrong, to put up boundaries that did not allow her father physically to touch her, and to feel safe enough to express some anger toward her parents in her therapist's office. Still, she had a long way to go. Even though Eileen's mind knew the abuse was not her fault, her physical and emotional reactions revealed deep shame and guilt. Her body still felt like her father's possession, polluted with her father's touch. Any pleasurable, sensual, or, most of all, sexual responses felt scary and inextricably connected to him. She was beginning to make a few friends her own age, but close relationships, even with the women in her order, were slow going.

It was at this point that Eileen came to an Opening to Grace Gestalt Pastoral Care workshop to see if she could discover a way to take the next steps toward healing. It seemed apparent to me that she had already explored much of her inner terrain and now had reached a plateau in her growth. After physically expressing some rage at her father with a plastic bat and pillow, Eileen seemed ready to lay claim to her own body.

After physically expressing some rage at her father with a plastic bat and pillow, Eileen seemed ready to lay claim to her own body.

When I proposed the idea of a special cleansing and claiming liturgy, Eileen loved the idea but imposed two conditions on the process. First, she said, no one would touch her unless she gave explicit permission. There would be no laying on of hands, no anointing, no supportive pats, no hugs. Second, although Eileen, a nun, is a devoutly committed Christian, no one would mention the name of Jesus during this special liturgy. She explained that when she got in touch with ancient father-induced feelings, Jesus' maleness invariably got confused with the maleness of her father. But she said "Christ" was okay with her. Somehow, for her, the name Christ seemed to transcend gender and sexuality.

I explained to the group that because things had been done to Eileen without her permission, it was especially urgent that Eileen have control of everything that would happen in her liturgy. I also pointed out that setting such clear limits was, in itself, a sign of enormous growth. Our all-woman group readily agreed to Eileen's terms, and I suggested that each person promise to honor Eileen's boundaries as part of our preparation and planning. Accordingly, we had a little "preliturgy" in which each person told Eileen, "I promise in the name of Christ that I will pray for you and support you while respecting your boundaries. I will name Christ as Lord, but I will not mention Jesus. I will not touch you in any way unless you invite me to. I will not say or do anything without first asking your permission."

At my suggestion Eileen practiced more boundary drawing as each person walked slowly toward her. When each one was as close as Eileen wanted, she said, "No!" At that signal each individual froze in place, not moving an inch. Eileen ordered several people to back up, and they obeyed immediately. Having her "no" instantly respected was new, exciting, and enormously healing for Eileen, and she wanted to repeat the exercise several times. This small bit of Gestalt work paved the way for the healing liturgy that was to follow.

Before we began I made it clear to Eileen that she could ask us to repeat or revise anything that would be said or done. She could ask us to pause whenever she wanted more time to take in what was happening. She could even stop us completely; all she had to do was say the word. Oddly, this explicit invitation to be in charge actually helped Eileen surrender more deeply to God and the healing process that emerged from her personal liturgy. As we planned together, we pondered how to do a cleansing liturgy without touch. Finally someone suggested that we flick water on her with a leafy branch dipped in a large bowl of water. Eileen liked the idea, and so it was settled.

Eileen wanted to be outdoors for her liturgy, "not trapped in a building or sitting in a chair." Accordingly, the liturgy took place on the deck of the house in which we were meeting. Eileen stood beside a small table that held the bowl of water and the leafy branch. The rest of us stood around her in a circle.

We began with prayer. We asked that God enable us to speak words of truth and power. We prayed that Eileen would be opened up to receive her liturgy into the deepest part of herself, and that God would work through our liturgy to heal. We also asked God to touch the bowl of water and make it a vehicle of God's cleansing and healing.

Then, with Eileen's permission, each person in turn spoke the truth to Eileen, truth she already knew well but was unable to let in. Notice that their words were rooted not in their opinions or in their personal liking for Eileen or their own reactions to her abuse, but in gospel certainties: God's love of Eileen, the goodness of God's creation, and God's desire to redeem and make new.

Although we had planned the general contours and guidelines of the liturgy of cleansing and claiming that followed our prayer, we had not written down the exact words that would be said. Instead, we tried to reach deep at each moment and, as best we could, speak from our own well of faith. All of us sprinkled Eileen as we spoke, and between each statement the ad hoc congregation responded with a fervent "Amen!" At Eileen's request we paused frequently and moved very slowly, asking her at every juncture if she was ready to continue. Eileen was weeping softly and breathing very deeply for most of the liturgy.

> *First person:* Eileen, I tell you in the name of Christ that your body never belonged to your father. In Christ, no person can own another. Your body belongs only to you and to the God who created you.
>
> *Eileen (weeping):* I claim that my body never belonged to my father. My body belongs only to me and to God.
>
> *First person:* With this water I cleanse away the distorted claim that your father owns your body.
>
> *Eileen:* That's true! My father does not own my body!
>
> *Second person:* Eileen, I tell you in the name of Christ that you have a right to say who may touch you, and how.
>
> *Eileen:* I affirm in the name of Christ that I really do have a right to say who will touch my body!
>
> *Second person:* With this water I wash away your father's distorted and abusive touching.

Eileen (still weeping): Oh, wow! That feels wonderful. Please sprinkle me again, and say those same words some more.

Second person: With this water I wash away your father's distorted and abusive touching . . . With this water I wash away your father's distorted and abusive touching . . .With this water I wash away your father's distorted and abusive touching . . . With this water I wash away your father's distorted and abusive touching.

Eileen (a mixture of deep, shuddering breaths; tears; and smiles)

Third person: Eileen, you have felt guilt and shame for what happened to you. I say to you in the name of Christ that it was never your fault.

Eileen: It was never my fault. It was never my fault! Oh my gosh, it really was never my fault!

Third person: With this water I cleanse you from false guilt and shame.

Eileen (still breathing deeply): Thank you, thank you. I feel like I'm sort of drinking in a new way of being.

Tilda: Eileen, can we give you some of this water to drink, so you can let your body physically drink in a new way of being?

Eileen: I would love that.

Tilda (handing her a glass of the water from the bowl): Eileen, here is cleansing, renewing water that has been blessed by God. Drink this in the faith that God is working to heal you. Drink in that it was never your fault. Drink in a new, more healed way of being.

Eileen (drinking thirstily): Ooh! . . . Ah! . . . This is so good!

Fourth person: Eileen, you have felt polluted and dirty because of what your father did to you. I tell you in the name of Christ that you need not carry your father's sin in your body any longer.

Eileen: I don't have to carry my father's sin in my body anymore. I really don't! Of course I don't!

Fourth person: With this water we cleanse away your feeling of interior pollution and filth. I declare in the name of Christ that you are clean and new, just as you were created to be. I bless and consecrate your body as holy and as a place where the Holy Spirit lives.

Eileen (grinning): Hey, I need you to stop sprinkling and start pouring. I want the whole bowl! I want to get soaked!

Fourth person (pours at least two quarts of water all over Eileen's body): Eileen, in the name of Christ, receive God's grace poured out for you! Remember your baptism and be thankful! And in the name of Christ we declare that your sensuality and sexuality are not connected to your father. In the name of Christ we claim this separation, and we say that your body was created by God to feel pleasure, and to rejoice in sexual responses as a gift of God. Remember, when God was creating the world, God kept saying, "That's good! That's good! That's good!"

Eileen (stands soaking wet in silence for several minutes, her face shining, still breathing deeply): Oh my gosh, I can't believe it. I feel new, like a baby. I'm not dirty anymore! I really am clean! My body belongs to me! And when I pictured my father just now, I saw him as very tiny, about as big as a toddler. This is the first time I've ever seen him like that, believe me! . . . I feel so wonderful. Thank you all so much.

After several moments of silence, I asked Eileen if she would like us to pray for her in thanksgiving and ask that the healing that had just occurred would be planted deeply in her. I asked if we could also pray for her parents' healing. I suggested that we could stretch our arms toward her, without touching, as a gesture of laying on of hands. She replied, "Oh yes, I want your prayers. And I can't believe I'm saying this, but I want you to put your hands on me. I want to experience goodness through my body. So please touch and pray." We did, and she did.

I called Eileen a few months later to find out how the liturgy had settled in her. She said, "I still feel so different, like my body is holy— and mine, just as we said in the liturgy. I feel very little guilt and shame these days. My therapy is going really well, and so is my prayer. I just feel God with me a lot more now. It was such a simple and profound thing we did. I think I would have never gotten to this point with therapy alone. I really needed that liturgy."

Four years later, I called Eileen to ask if I could write her story. She readily agreed, saying, "I know that we are never finished growing, and healing is a process, but that liturgy opened up a very deep healing that changed my life. I often go back to that night in my head and in my prayer. I can still feel the water and the love. Maybe most healing for me was the intermingling of the healing water and my tears. They were one, and I saw that they couldn't be separated.

"I also learned more deeply what support and community is. I continue to be impressed by the authority of communal prayer to evoke the presence of the Holy Spirit."

Eileen was right. She wasn't finished growing. Her story continues below.

Eileen's Celebration: Making Vows and Taking a New Name

Eileen, the nun whose cleansing liturgy was just described, received a second healing liturgy eight years later. In those eight years she had earned an advanced theological degree with academic distinction, completed a training program for hospital chaplains, and held a demanding job in ministry. Right after her first liturgy, she began weekly sessions of Gestalt Pastoral Care.

Although her cleansing and claiming liturgy had been "powerfully healing" and had "changed everything," she soon found that all the emotional residue of her severe trauma was not magically gone. The liturgy, which had been so instrumental in healing her shame, seemed to free her to take the plunge into other pain stemming from her abuse. Eileen cried more ancient, unshed tears. She discovered her own fierce protectiveness and love for the little girl she once was. She physically expressed her rage at her father in my office before letting it go. She relied on grace to enter into the difficult process of forgiveness.

Eileen made rapid progress. As time went on, her father's abuse had less and less power to derail her as she felt his influence wane. When she stopped weekly Gestalt Pastoral Care two years later, she was feeling happy, self-confident, spiritually alive, and profoundly grateful for the healing power of Christ. She easily maintained this good balance for five years.

Then Eileen was given a highly responsible role in her religious order that necessitated moving far away from New York City and a job she loved. Besides having to learn the ropes of a new ministry, she found herself working with another sister whose personal style was quite different from hers. She sorely missed the rich cultural diversity and excitement of New York City and experienced her new geographic location as not only too hot but achingly desolate. Most of all, Eileen grieved the rich network of dear friendships she had left behind.

Soon after this unsettling move, she began to feel stressed and a bit anxious, then sad, then downright depressed. To her horror, she even began to think of suicide. "Not that I would really do it," she said, "but the thoughts are there." Wisely she sought help. She shared her struggle with the nuns with whom she now lived and asked them to pray for her. A psychiatrist gave her medication, and Eileen began seeing a therapist in her new city. She and her colleague in ministry had some sessions with a therapist/supervisor. Since Eileen and I had worked together before, she called me to arrange for some phone sessions as well.

Soon things began to change. Eileen and her colleague ironed out their difficulties and became firm and trusting friends. She found that she could be both competent and compassionate in her new ministry. The medication kicked in, and her depression faded. Other new friendships sprouted. She began to adjust to the climate and the lack of urban stimulation. Her prayer flowed more easily. She just felt better all around, with one important exception: she still had thoughts of suicide. This, even though she was not acting self-destructively at all. On the contrary, she was taking extraordinary measures to care for her spiritual and emotional health.

As we talked, it became clear that suicide was a sort of "ace up her sleeve," something to fall back on if things got really bad. As long as suicide was a possibility—no matter how remote—she would always have an out. As much as she wanted to get rid of these thoughts, she had to admit that the possibility of suicide brought a measure of comfort and security. She never again wanted to feel as terrible as she did just before she began to work on her childhood rapes.

Immediately Eileen saw that she was putting her trust in something other than God. Unwittingly, she had erected an idol. After a week of much prayer and honest soul-searching, she decided to surrender the ace up her sleeve. She was ready, with God's help, to put all her trust in God once again. This she did, praying aloud on the phone so that I could witness this wrenching and life-giving prayer in which she renounced suicide as an option. She finished sweaty and exhausted but feeling good about what she had just done.

By the next week she was immersed in Love that would not let her go and living in such profound joy that she could hardly contain herself. She said, "I can't imagine any more joy than I have now. I don't think I will live much longer, because how could there be anything more for me in this life than this incredible joy? This is very different from suicide! I just feel that my life is somehow complete. But," she said with a laugh, "I know that God often surprises me with more than I can imagine."

Soon God's newest surprise was revealed: the rebirth of "Phoebe," her secret name for the joyful, strong, beautiful, innocent, playful, free, smart, and feisty child she was before the rapes began. Somehow as Eileen surrendered her idol, Phoebe (which means "light" or "radiance") became a vital part of the adult woman. When Eileen stopped holding on to the possibility of death by suicide, she simply burst into bloom.

As Phoebe became a more integrated part of Eileen, we started to imagine a liturgy in which she could celebrate her new healing. The liturgy would include a formal rededication of her vows as a nun, and some new personal vows that would refer to her surrender of the ace up her sleeve. As a symbol of her healing, she would claim liturgically the wonderful reality of Phoebe and ask some dear friends to call her by that name.

The liturgy took place in my office at a time when Eileen and the sister who was her new colleague in ministry were in New York to attend a meeting. Another nun, Eileen's dearest friend from New York, was also glad to be there. The four of us gathered around a small table covered with a white cloth. I provided a Celtic cross for the table, and anointing oil. Eileen brought a small piece of handwoven fabric, a special candle, and a plant that had belonged to her mother. Two friends who could not attend loaned a religious medal and a small sculpture, symbols of their prayers and spiritual presence, and these objects were placed on the table as well. On a side table was a pitcher of hot water and a basin filled with rolled-up washcloths for foot washing. Eileen and I had done some planning on the phone, but Eileen had put her liturgy into final form and brought with her a carefully worded order of worship, which included parts for each of us to lead. She titled her personal liturgy "Welcome to Phoebe."

When Eileen stopped holding on to the possibility of death by suicide, she simply burst into bloom.

The simple liturgy began with a reading of Romans 16:1. I read Paul's words:

> "I commend to you our sister Phoebe, a deacon of the church . . . so that you may welcome her in the Lord as is fitting for the saints, and help her in whatever she may require from you, for she has been a benefactor of many and of myself as well."

After a brief introduction, someone read Psalm 139, and we listened to a CD and read a poem that held special meaning for Eileen.

Next, Eileen told in some detail the story of her healing. Even though each of us knew much of the story, it was important for

Eileen to give witness to what God had done for her, formally intro-
duce us to Phoebe, and explain why she was claiming Phoebe as a
new name.

Each of us then anointed and blessed Eileen, called her Phoebe
for the first time, and promised to support her as she continued her
healing journey. Phoebe, radiant and smiling hugely, stood and read
her vows slowly and reverently. We could sense the shimmering presence of the Holy Spirit as Phoebe joyfully rededicated her whole
being to God.

Here are the momentous vows—old and new—that Phoebe
made that day:

> Loving God, source of all mercy and compassion, in the presence of
> this ecumenical gathering of sisters in religious community and sis-
> ters in ministry, I renew the vows I made at my profession in [her reli-
> gious community] and consecrate my entire life to you anew.
>
> With a heartfelt sense of deeper freedom and gratitude for my life and
> for the new life given me, I respond to a call to name myself Phoebe
> and commit myself once again to a life of celibate chastity, acknowl-
> edging you as my first and all-encompassing love. I give myself in that
> same love to my sisters in community, to people in need of healing
> love and understanding, and to my family and friends.
>
> I recommit myself to a life of evangelical poverty, striving to live sim-
> ply and to seek unity of mind and heart, sharing all that I have and
> who I am.
>
> I recommit myself to a life of obedience within [her religious com-
> munity]. I desire to inform my mind, prepare my heart for dialogue,
> listen to others in love, and accept your call to conversion of heart.
>
> I recommit myself to a life of service through the works of mercy.
> Enriched by your love and healed by your mercy, I will serve those
> who suffer in poverty, illness, or are crushed by life-sapping social
> structures.
>
> Birthed to life through the womb of your holy people gathered here
> today, and those afar who support me in spirit and in prayer, people

who have loved and cared for me, I, Phoebe, vow to reverence, cherish, and honor the life you have given me. In gratitude for this gift and the call to life I hear deep in my heart's core, I vow and promise to care for my body and love the flesh you have given me by carefully tending to what is good and wholesome for my body. I vow and promise to enrich my heart and spirit through prayer, music, study, and contemplation. I commit my energy to what is whole, holy, and life giving in our world.

Dependent always on your grace and mercy, I surrender to you, Loving Source of my life, my memory, my understanding, and my whole will, all that I am and possess and all that I may be. I rely on your unconditional love for me to empower me to choose daily to surrender to you my hidden shame—the ace up my sleeve. I beg to live simply by faith and ask that this attraction to death, sorrow, and self-destruction be continuously purified by your transforming mercy, leading me to the light and life you set before me every day.

I vow to care for and protect Phoebe as your loving child, whose life you welcome, bless, and honor through the presence of Sister _____ and Sister _____ , and Tilda Norberg, accompanied in spirit and in prayer by Sister _____ and Dr. _____ .

I ask for the grace to fulfill these vows, renewed and made anew today, the 14th of September, 2006.

Phoebe's religious community has a tradition of signing a copy of solemn vows in the presence of its religious superior, who also signs the document. In accordance with this custom, Phoebe formally signed her vows, and the three of us signed as witnesses. As soon as she returned home, she would ask the two who were present in spirit to add their signatures.

After singing a hymn from the Taizé community, accompanied by me on the viola, the service concluded with foot washing as a sign of our shared servant ministry and our shared call to allow Jesus to wash our feet, that is, to touch parts of us that are in need of healing.

A week later, Phoebe shared her reactions to her personal liturgy. Her comments reflected both her profound understanding of the role liturgy can play in healing, and that healing is a process that continues until death. She said, "Right after I got home from New York, one of the younger sisters said to me that my trip to New York must have been really good, because I seemed different to her. I surely know I am different, more assertive, less wimpish, more able to ask for what I need. I know, of course, that I will have bad days, and that more healing will be needed. I also have faith that that more healing will come."

Within weeks more healing did come. Phoebe said,

"The other day I told someone the big secret, that I was sexually abused by my father. I just said it casually, like it was simply factual. There was no emotional load around my statement, no anger or shame or bitterness. Then I sensed God saying, "It's okay to let all that go." And I have let it go. I really sense a shift to a whole new level of forgiveness of my father and a deep reclaiming of all of who I am. In a funny way, my father doesn't matter anymore. His power over me has been broken. I honestly think I'm finished with him.

"I also notice that the liturgy—the foot washing and my new name and the anointing—are still becoming more of a lived reality. My ministry is already enriched and deepened as I am able to be present with more of myself, and share more of who I am. Phoebe is a big help to Eileen!

"I felt so authentic and truly present to the vows. I really felt that this was my first profession, although I entered the community at age seventeen and was professed as a nun years ago. Back then my profession was made of goodwill, hope, and desire but with little freedom and self-knowledge. Now, after forty-three years in community, I remade my vows in genuine freedom. I know I am called by grace, and by grace I make a life choice for the rest of my life. In our community when we die, we are buried with the vows we signed at our profession. When I die—whenever that is—I want to be buried with these new vows.

"I see that both personal liturgies helped me solidify a reality I had already experienced. Both marked an honest moment of conversion in my life, and I know I will need more conversions in the future. Both times I had a sense of myself as more truly who I am called to be, and

I will continue to find out how God will keep on shaping me. Both liturgies were just beautiful graces, and God was surely present with us. I am very grateful."

The story of Eileen/Phoebe gives magnificent witness to God's desire to make all things new. Healing prayer, hard inner work, pastoral care, medical help, friendships, psychotherapy, ministry supervision, religious community and wider church support, surrender to calls within her larger vocation as a nun, and her active consent to the grace that called for continual growth—all contributed to Eileen/Phoebe's healing.

Of course, the two liturgies were also a vital part of her healing process. These significant and memorable landmark events celebrated healing already accomplished; provided a venue for telling stories and witnessing vows; made time for focused healing prayer; acknowledged the support of the church; became personal icons that summed up God's work in her; and, through God's grace, were themselves powerful agents of growth and healing.

I pray that you, too, like the many people whose stories are told in this book, will discover for yourself that God works to heal and nurture growth through simple liturgies tailored to fit just one person at a time.

Appendix

Naming Lies,
Speaking the Truth
A Brief Guide for a Liturgical Process

Preparation

1. Explain that the way we are treated, life circumstances, and direct admonitions—especially in childhood—can give us ideas about ourselves, about the world, and about God that are simply not true. However, they *feel* true and thus have great power to stunt our lives and cause great suffering. We in the gathered church have authority to speak the truth with power. Explain that in this healing liturgy we will identify the lies one person has borne, and will speak the gospel truth to that person in a liturgical way, relying on God to give us the words and to bring the healing.

Make sure the recipient knows that she can interrupt to catch her breath, ask for different words or actions, ask that something be repeated, or for any other reason. If she wants, she can stop the liturgy of lies and truth completely. Everyone should understand that the person being prayed for has final say about what will or will not happen. This liturgy should not be coercive or condemning in any way.

2. Pray that God will direct the process and empower members of the gathered church to speak the truth in a way that can be heard by the person receiving prayer.

3. Ask the recipient to tell the story that underlies the need for healing. Learn how the recipient came to feel that his or her lies are truth.

4. Work together as a group to make or modify a list of the lies the person was taught, either by circumstances, or by what someone did or said. List the lies on a chalkboard or on newsprint. Be sure to list only statements that express something about the personhood of the recipient. This important step ensures that the statements listed are actually lies.

So, for example, if a person lists as a lie, *"My father didn't love me enough to stay with our family,"* the leader needs to point out that though Dad actually left, no one can know how much he loved or didn't love. Work to clarify the lie underneath the experiences. The lie emerging from this experience might be, for example, *"I'm not lovable."* Other examples:

"People get scared when you express your emotions." This admonition, learned in childhood, is not a lie, because someone may indeed get scared of another's strong feelings, and in this particular recipient's family, that was actually the case. The real lie shifts the focus to a false and stultifying demand about how the recipient needs to live: *"You have to suppress your feelings so no one will be scared of you."* In other words, the lie is expressed not as, "People will think . . ." but as, "You should be . . ."

"If you just tried harder, you could be a better mom." This statement is not a lie, for who couldn't improve in some way? The leader perceived, however, that the real lie behind this statement was, *"You should be a perfect mom."* When this wording was suggested, the recipient agreed immediately.

5. Instruct the gathered church about speaking the truth. You might say, "Remember, the only truth you speak here is based on the gospel, not on your opinion or your reaction to the story of the recipient or what you imagine the recipient might want to hear. For example, don't say, "Even though your mother treated you badly, I'm sure she really loved you." Instead say something like:

> "I believe that even during your terrible childhood, God was present, loving you, treasuring you. I remember how the Bible says, 'I will never leave you or forsake you.' I believe this is true, and I proclaim this message to you in the name of Christ."

If possible, refer to scripture each time, not in a proof-texting way but as a way to underscore your own Christian faith. Each member of the gathered church can take a turn doing this, or one person can do most of the talking and the others respond with "Amen."

6. Ask the recipient if she would like to be anointed with oil or splashed with water as part of the liturgy, or if she has some other idea of her own that seems important to include. Find out by what names she might like to hear God addressed.

The Liturgical Action

In this liturgy each of the lies is formally identified as a lie, followed by the gospel truth that counteracts the lie. Thus, the flow of the service might go something like this:

Each member of the gathered church in turn draws a cross on the person's forehead and speaks such words as:

> "_____ [name], I anoint you for healing in the name of God the Father, Jesus the Son, and the Holy Spirit. "

or

> "I anoint you for healing in the name of the Creator, the Redeemer, and the Sanctifier."

Or, the gathered church says some other words that "speak the language" of the person being prayed for.

If the recipient prefers not to be anointed, each participant from the ad hoc church might simply take the recipient's hand, and say something like:

"_____ [name], I'm praying for your healing in the name of God the Father, Jesus the Son, and the Holy Spirit."

Next, the participant names a lie, saying, for example:

"_____, you have been taught that _____ [e.g, "You are no good"]. I proclaim to you in the name of Jesus Christ that this is a lie."

The ad hoc church responds: **Amen!**

Then the participant speaks the truth, a brief gospel response to that particular lie, including, if possible, a reference to scripture. For example:

"The truth is _____ [e.g, 'You are of infinite worth to God. I believe God holds you in the palm of God's hand. Jesus loves you tenderly and delights in the fact you are alive.']."

The church responds: **Amen!**

Make sure to allow time after each declaration for the recipient to react or respond. Remind the recipient to breathe in each new truth. Don't go on until the recipient is ready. Be comfortable with tears if she or he should cry. Tears are often a natural part of this liturgical practice.

When the list of lies is finished, lay hands on the person and pray for her if she so desires. Pray especially that the truth will find a home in her heart.

Notes

Introduction

1. For a compendium of liturgies for special needs and occasions, see *Healing Liturgies for the Seasons of Life* by Abigail Rian Evans (Louisville, KY: Westminster John Knox Press, 2005).

2. Opening to Grace weekend healing retreats are a basic venue for Gestalt Pastoral Care, a combination of Gestalt work, healing prayer, and spiritual companioning. Opening to Grace retreats are limited to six participants and two or three observers and intercessors. Each participant has the opportunity to work with his or her growth process with the support and prayers of the ad hoc church. Although each person is offered a great deal of spaciousness to choose how deeply he or she will participate, these retreats tend to be fairly intensive. Most people experience them as important times of healing. For more information, see pages 190–91.

Chapter 1

1. This story was first told in *Consenting to Grace: An Introduction to Gestalt Pastoral Care* (Staten Island, NY: Penn House Press, 2006), 107–8.

2. See *Consenting to Grace*, chapter 9, pages 142–61, for a more complete explanation of Gestalt Pastoral Care experiments.

3. For insight into this healing story, I am indebted to Dr. Robert Webber, professor emeritus of New Testament at Lancaster Theological Seminary, who presented these ideas when we taught a class together many years ago.

Chapter 3

1. For a discussion of how to assist someone in the process of forgiveness, see *Consenting to Grace*, pages 82–87.

2. Matthew 11:30, NIV.

Chapter 5

1. Remember that all depressions are different and have many different causes, such as chemical imbalance, trauma, repressed anger, or even boredom. Most people can't leave a major depression behind just by deciding to do so, and this story was not written to make you feel guilty for what you can't help. On the other hand, it is worth asking if even the smallest part of you is clinging to an old and familiar way of living.

Stories of Personal Healing Liturgies

1. This class is part of the Certificate Program of Rising Hope, Inc., which is taught by volunteers at seven New York state correctional facilities. Begun as an offshoot of New York Theological Seminary in 1995, the program is a full-time, college-level, academic commitment for prisoners. Inmates take classes in biblical studies, theology, sociology of religious institutions, comparative religion, church history, ethics, social work, and pastoral care. Upon a prisoner's release, the program may translate into about a year of col-

lege credits, depending on where the student applies to continue his college education.

2. Dora and Ralph's "Service of Endings and Beginnings" was inspired by a book titled *Ritual in a New Day: An Invitation* (Nashville, TN: Abingdon Press, 2006), a project of the Alternative Rituals Project of the Section on Worship of the Board of Discipleship of the United Methodist Church. The committee that created the book was called the Task Force on the Cultural Context of Ritual, chaired by Jeanne Audrey Powers, then assistant general secretary of the Ecumenical and Interreligious Concerns Division of the United Methodist Board of Global Ministries. See the section titled "Rituals for Endings and Beginnings," pages 97–126.

3. Barbara's story was first told in abbreviated form in *Consenting to Grace*, page 123.

4. Dave's story is reprinted from *Consenting to Grace*, pages 121–22.

Bibliography and Resources

Book of Blessings: Ritual Edition. Collegeville, MN: Liturgical Press, 1989. Contains the approved English translation of *De Benedictionibus* prepared by the International Commission on English in the Liturgy, as well as forty-two orders and prayers of blessing prepared by the Committee on the Liturgy of the National Conference of Catholic Bishops and approved for use in the dioceses of the United States of America.

The Book of Occasional Services, 2006 (Episcopal Church USA). New York: Church Publishing, 2006.

Evans, Abigail Rian. *Healing Liturgies for the Seasons of Life.* Louisville, KY: Westminster John Knox Press, 2005.

InterLutheran Worship Commission, comp. *Occasional Services.* Minneapolis: Augsburg Fortress, Publishers, 2004.

Langford, Andy, ed. *The United Methodist Book of Worship.* Nashville, TN: Abingdon Press, 1992.

Langhauser, Susan. *Blessings and Rituals for the Journey of Life.* Nashville, TN: Abingdon Press, 2000. This book offers pastors a collection of ready-made, easily adaptable blessings and rituals for a variety of occasions. It contains four major chapters: "Children," "Adults," "Everyday Life," and "Pastoral Care."

Norberg, Tilda. *Consenting to Grace: An Introduction to Gestalt Pastoral Care*. Staten Island, NY: Penn House Press, 2006.

Schroeder, Celeste. *Embodied Prayer: Harmonizing Body and Soul*. Ligouri, MO: Liguori Publications, 1995.

Willimon, William H. *Worship as Pastoral Care*. Nashville, TN: Abingdon Press, 1982.

Thomas Duncan Photography

About the Author

⤫

Tilda Norberg, a United Methodist minister, is the founder of Gestalt Pastoral Care. For more information about Gestalt Pastoral Care, see pages 190–91.

Norberg is the author of *Consenting to Grace: An Introduction to Gestalt Pastoral Care; Ashes Transformed: Healing from Trauma;* and *Threadbear: A Story of Christian Healing for Adult Survivors of Sexual Abuse.* She is the coauthor, with Robert Webber, of *Stretch Out Your Hand: Exploring Healing Prayer.*

Norberg is a graduate of Union Theological Seminary in New York City, The Gestalt Institute of Canada, and the Lomi School in San Francisco. She and her husband, the Reverend George McClain, live on Staten Island and are the parents of two grown children, Shana and Noah, and the proud grandparents of Silas Norberg Bodah.

Other Titles of Interest

All of these books except *Consenting to Grace* are available by calling 1-800-027-0433 or by visiting www.upperroom.org/bookstore.

Ashes Transformed
Healing from Trauma
43 Stories of Faith
by Tilda Norberg

This book witnesses to the power of God to heal persons from even the worst tragedies. Norberg writes, "Painful experiences, no matter how catastrophic, can be healed through a combination of inner work and prayer. You do not forget the experiences, but they no longer have the power to terrify you and control your reactions." This book is worth the price alone for its beautiful healing prayers.
ISBN 978-0-8358-0986-3 • Paperback • 192 pages

Stretch Out Your Hand
Exploring Healing Prayer
by Tilda Norberg and Robert D. Webber

Stretch Out Your Hand suggests that healing is not just getting well from an illness, but a beautiful, dynamic process leading to the wholeness that God wills for us. Through their candid writing style, the authors address tough questions and offer practical ways for readers to consider the varieties of God's healing love for individuals, institutions, and communities.
ISBN 978-0-0872-9 • Paperback • 144 pages

Stretch Out Your Hand Leader's Guide
ISBN 978-0-8358-0870-5 • Paperback • 48 pages

Cultivating Christian Community
by Thomas R. Hawkins

Hawkins offers readers a vision of what Christian community could be. He identifies practices that help small groups cultivate Christian community through listening, dialogue, discernment, covenant making, prayer and reflection, and hospitality.
ISBN 978-0-88177-327-9 • Paperback • 112 pages

Patterned by Grace
How Liturgy Shapes Us
by Daniel T. Benedict Jr.

Patterned by Grace rekindles the discovery of worship as a remarkable spiritual adventure. This book examines the hidden rhythms of Sunday worship, Holy Communion, baptism, daily prayer (the daily office), and the liturgical year. The exercises in the group discussion guide at the back of the book awaken the reader's imagination to the power of liturgical life.
ISBN 978-0-8358-9905-5 • Paperback • 160 pages

Consenting to Grace
An Introduction to Gestalt Pastoral Care
by Tilda Norberg

Set in the context of the author's own healing journey, *Consenting to Grace* integrates healing prayer, spiritual companioning, and insights from Gestalt psychotherapy. Norberg teaches those in ministry how to pay closer and more holistic attention to each person. She suggests many wise and practical ways to helps others "consent to grace," that is, to welcome the specific healing and growth God offers at every moment. *Note:* To order this book, visit www.gestaltpastoralcare.com.

About Gestalt Pastoral Care

Tilda Norberg worked her way toward the synthesis that became Gestalt Pastoral Care (GPC) out of her need to pull together parts of her own life: the impossibility of finding a position in ministry as a woman after her ordination in 1968; her subsequent training and private practice in Gestalt psychotherapy; and later, a scary call to healing ministry. GPC developed slowly as her integration became clearer. She is still astonished to find that she has been given much more than healing for herself; here was a brand-new call to a unique ministry that seemed to meet the longing of many church folk for physical, emotional, and spiritual healing.

In 1984 three other clergywomen took Tilda to lunch and asked her to show them how to offer pastoral care in this new way. There a training program that still continues was born. Along the way Gestalt Pastoral Care Ecumenical Associates was formed to offer expanded training; Opening to Grace workshops; and church retreats on specialized topics such as faith imagination, listening to God in your dreams, healing liturgies, and healing from sexual abuse.

GPC is a model of healing ministry that integrates Gestalt growth work, Christian spiritual companioning, and healing prayer. It rests on the conviction that God is already bringing some kind of healing and wholeness to those who come for help. Always there is a call to grow, to change, to become more whole, more like Jesus.

GPC is holistic, experiential, gentle, and nonanalytical. Seldom does *talking about* or *figuring out* occur in GPC; instead, close attention is paid to the moment-by-moment process of the person seeking growth. The goal is to cooperate as best we can with what the Holy Spirit seems to be stirring up. Gestalt "experiments"— a physical, emotional, or spiritual action in response to present awareness— help foster more awareness and move the process along. There is no pushing, only suggesting; no one is ever urged to do anything he or she does not want to do. The urgency comes from God whispering inside the person who wants to grow. Most sessions include laying on of hands and prayer for healing.

What people say about GPC:

What I learned in GPC is immediately available as I do spiritual direction. It has enriched my pastoral practice immensely, and I had twenty-three years of experience before I took the course. Wow! Why didn't I know of this before?

— A Roman Catholic priest

After seven years of graduate school, one day of working with GPC totally changed the way I work with people.

— A psychotherapist

This class [in GPC] is the best thing that ever happened to me. It's just amazing to experience how healing happens just naturally if we don't do anything to mess it up.

— A prison inmate

I have had a new experience of Jesus. This is really something.

— A pastor nearing retirement

For more information, training opportunities, and workshop schedules, e-mail tildanorberg@yahoo.com or visit the Web site: www.gestaltpastoralcare.com.